TGV

HANDBOOK

BRIAN PERREN

Capital Transport

First published 1993

ISBN 185414 161 9

Published by Capital Transport Publishing
38 Long Elmes, Harrow Weald, Middlesex

Printed by Winchmore Press, Ilford, Essex

The front cover photo is of a Bordeaux–Paris TGV near Châtellerault in August 1992. *M J Collins*

The front cover inset is of a Eurostar train at Folkestone. *Colin J Marsden*

The back cover photo is of Sud Est stock at the Paris maintenance depot. *GEC Alsthom*

Contents

Despite the 6 to 7-hour journey time, TGV is a popular mode of travel between Paris and the resort towns on the Côte D'Azur. Bound for Paris this single-unit service is threading its way round the sinuous curves along the coast between Mandelieu-la-Napoule and Théoule-sur-Mer. Brian Perren

Atlantique set on an afternoon cross-country service from Lyon to Tours shown here north of Mâcon-Loché station. Brian Perren

1. Routes: Lignes à Grande Vitesse

Looking back to 27 September 1981, when the first (southern) section of the Paris-Sud Est Ligne à Grande Vitesse opened for public service, few could have visualised the extent to which high-speed rail travel would evolve during the ensuing 12 years.

Today the Paris Sud Est (PSE) train fleet covers a network of 2,560 km (1,591 miles), of which 455 km (283 miles) is new purpose-built high-speed railway. When the line opened in 1981, just 12 cities and towns were served. Today the PSE serves 50 towns – increasing to 60 during the skiing season – with a total of 30 million inhabitants. TGV is more than a technical achievement. In 1991 more than 20 million people travelled on the PSE on journeys which totalled 11 billion passenger-kilometres. Average use is 55,000 persons per day, a load factor of 80%. The record daily use was 93,400 persons on 7 March 1992. In 10 years total traffic on the PSE has increased by 90%. This has generated an internal financial rate of return of about 15% for SNCF – but the social-benefit figure is of the order of 30%. The PSE project – which cost FFr 18 billion at 1989 values – was self-funded by SNCF.

Traffic growth on the PSE route has exceeded all expectations giving SNCF the confidence to build other routes creating the core of the emerging European high-speed rail network. We have seen the completion and successful launch of

Just north of Mâcon-Loché station northbound TGVs start the 15 km 3.5% climb to the summit at Col du Bois Clair. Brian Perren

the Atlantique route linking Paris and the West and South West of France. Nord Europe is almost complete and work is well underway on the Paris Inter-connexion and Rhône Alpes projects. By 1995 SNCF will have a fleet of over 300 TGV trainsets to serve these routes.

Today's high-speed trains routinely travel at 300 km/h (186 mph), but the research which has made such speeds possible was started in the 1950s. With large sections of newly-electrified routes funded as part of its post-World War 2 recovery plans, SNCF initiated a programme of technical research. The purpose was to determine the performance characteristics of electric locomotives and coaches, the efficiency of current supply systems and the ability of overhead line equipment and electric sub-stations to cope with greatly increased levels of current consumption. This initial programme was concluded in 1955 when locomotives BB 9004 and CC 7107 achieved new world record speeds of 331 km/h (205.6 mph) on 28 and 29 March of that year.

Although line speeds on the principal French routes were raised to 160 km/h (100 mph) where conditions were suitable, it was not until May 1967 that trains timed to run at much greater speeds were introduced into public service between Paris and Toulouse. As well as providing special coaches with greater braking potential, it was also necessary to modify the existing signalling system so that the new 200 km/h (125 mph) trains could cohabit with slower trains without affecting the basic safety of the service. Encouraged by the success of these services, other 200 km/h services were introduced between Paris and Bordeaux. Initially these trains were only available to First Class passengers with payment of a substantial supplement.

However, in the 1970s the travel market had started to change. Package tours to more adventurous destinations and the growing ownership of private cars had created a mass travel market where passenger expectations were raised. Like other European railways, SNCF realised that much more needed to be done if rail travel was to be made more attractive for ordinary customers. Following extensive market research, SNCF launched a major revamp of its long-distance services: timetables were reorganised, stations were refurbished and over 3,000 new air-conditioned 'Corail' coaches were ordered and brought into service. With skilful marketing – and particular emphasis on customer care and special facilities – SNCF successfully established itself in the mass travel market. A secure business base for TGV had been established.

Paris-Sud Est

The decision to build the PSE line from Paris to Lyon evolved from two basic factors – the recognition by SNCF that rail could only remain competitive with the growing *autoroute* network and improved airline services if centre-to-centre journey times were drastically reduced, and the fact that even with modest rates of growth capacity on key strategic routes it would be unable to cope with expected future levels of business.

While significant sections of the Paris–Bordeaux line had a potential speed of 200 km/h and even higher, this was not the case on the classic Paris–Lyon–Méditerranée (PLM) route. Serving 40% of the entire population of France, the PLM is a route of major strategic importance. As well as serving Dijon, Lyon, Avignon and Marseille, it provides access to the French Alps, Switzerland (Lausanne) via Vallorbe, Geneva via Mâcon and Italy via Modane. By the start of the 1970s, a situation had developed where continuing growth of around 4% per year had led to the realisation that the route would soon be saturated to the extent that further growth and future levels of business would be constrained by route capacity.

There were two factors – track capacity and line speeds. For the greater part of its 315 km (196 miles) route from Paris to Dijon the PLM has four tracks, but there are two critical two-track sections between St Florentin and Les Laumes (83 km/52 miles) and Blaisy Bas to Dijon (26 km/16 miles) where pathing 160 km/h passenger trains and slower moving freights had become very difficult. While there were long sections of route fit for 160 km/h, the topography and track geometry was such as to rule out major infrastructure upgrading except at prohibitive cost. Also, the cost of doubling the 4 km (2.5 mile) Blaisy Bas Tunnel and the two-track section down into Dijon was not a practical possibility. Even though the route had been electrified for a little over 10 years, its practical operating capacity would soon be reached.

Given the impossibility of upgrading the PLM, SNCF prepared plans for a new high-speed railway which would link Paris, Dijon, Lyon and South East France. The cost of the new line was equal to about 40% of the cost of upgrading the PLM where this was theoretically possible. With almost all long-distance traffic transferred to the new line, ample capacity would then be available for freight and other lower-speed traffic.

However, unlike the Japanese Shinkansen which is a purpose-built self-contained system, the PSE line was designed as an increment to and part of the existing national network. Thus, after passage of the high speed line the new TGV trains would be able to run through to all other parts of the SNCF (electrified) system. Not only would this obviate the enormous environmental disturbance and cost of building new tracks into the centre of Paris, Lyon and other cities, but all of South East France would benefit from reduced journey times. This concept has been applied to all subsequent TGV projects.

Thanks to the ability of modern electric traction to cope with gradients as severe as 3.5% (1 in 28.5) and the capacity of low-slung rolling stock to sustain high standards of ride comfort through the curvature of modern track, the choice of an unobtrusive route through the French countryside was not too difficult. In fact, it is now possible for railway engineers to work within similar parameters as motorway builders. In 1969 a study group was formed to consider the practicalities of combining railway and road infrastructure where this was possible. For 60 or so kilometres the A5 *autoroute* runs alongside the PSE southwards from Melun, the Lyon Contournement follows the A432 and, as described later, TGV Nord Europe follows the Al *Autoroute du Nord*.

Work on the PSE line was started at the end of 1976 and completed in two stages – the southern section from Sathonay/Aisy to St-Florentin in September 1981 and the northern section from St-Florentin to Lieusaint in September 1983.

Designed for a potential speed of 300 km/h but currently operating at a maximum of 270 km/h (168 mph), the Ligne à Grande Vitesse starts at Lieusaint 29 km (18.3 miles) from Gare-de-Lyon terminus at Paris. From Lieusaint the route runs through open country, across the plain of Brie, but avoiding the towns of Montereau and Sens. At St-Florentin – 115 km (71.5 miles) from the start of the line at Lieusaint – there is a high-speed junction at the interface of the new line and the PLM line. From 1981 to 1983, before the whole line was open, this junction was used by TGVs to join the PLM line to/from Paris.

At Pasilly, 45 km (30 miles) beyond St-Florentin, the branch to Aisy parts company with the main line on turnouts designed for 220 km/h (137 mph). This short 15 km (9.3 miles) spur is the route for TGV trains to Dijon and thence through Dôle to Vallorbe and Switzerland. The first of only two intermediate stations is at Le Creusot-Montchanin (274 km/170 miles) from the start of the line and the second is at Mâcon-Loché (334 km / 207 miles). Just beyond Mâcon TGV station and before the railway crosses the River Sâone, there are single track connections onto the PLM line; the first of these enables postal TGVs from Paris

This **PSE** train is approaching the northern end of the **Sud Est** high-speed line at Lieusaint where the driver will lower the pantograph for the changeover from 25 to 1.5 kV power supplies and will switch off the cab-signalling system replacing it with the normal standard system for the remainder of the journey into Paris. The marker-boards on the left of the picture advise the driver to prepare to changeover to cab-signalling and alter his radio channel. Brian Perren

To accommodate the Paris Sud Est TGV service, substantial alterations were made to the track layout, signalling, platforms and passenger facilities at the Gare-de-Lyon terminal station in Paris. This Sud Est service is about to join the southbound main line heading for Lieusaint alongside a double-deck outer-suburban train which has just left a low-level terminal station platform. SNCF

to serve the Post Office station and the second is an emergency connection from the Lyon (TGV) direction onto the northbound PLM line towards Paris. Just to the east of the River Sâone viaduct at Mâcon is the second junction leading to Pont-de-Veyle and the classic line to Bourg-en-Bresse, Geneva and the French Alps. As originally built, the PSE line finishes at Sathonay, 393.8 km/244.7 miles from Lieusaint, which is 52 km (32 miles) beyond the Savoie Junction. Partly because the most suitable alignment into the Lyon area was through Sathonay and also because the increase in traffic necessitated a major reorganisation of train working through the Greater Lyon area, a major new station was built at Part-Dieu to cope with the volume of TGV traffic. Although the route is designed for 300 km/h, the present maximum speed is 270 km/h. As originally installed, the TVM 300 cab-signalling – described in Chapter 4 – gives an operating headway of five minutes. Power supplies are 25 kV ac.

The Atlantique Line

While work on the Atlantique project as a follow-on from the PSE lines began as early as 1975, it was SNCF's third rather than its second choice of route. Had agreement to build the Channel Tunnel been made earlier, TGV Nord Europe would have been the next to be built. By 1982, the SNCF Board of Directors had approved the Atlantique project and had submitted the proposals for Government approval; this was received on 1 July 1982 and the 'Public Utility' process was initiated. As a 'Declaration of Public Utility' gives wide powers to a state-owned concern – such as the compulsory purchase of land – the consultation process is very thorough but shorter than is the case in Britain and Germany. TGV Atlantique was declared a 'Public Utility' on 25 May 1984.

Like the PSE project, the case for the Atlantique line was based on the inability of the existing infrastructure out of Paris (Montparnasse) towards Le Mans and from Paris (Austerlitz) towards Orléans and Tours to cope with future levels of growth. Not only would the cost of upgrading these two routes be very high, but 200 km/h would have been the maximum speed which could have been achieved.

Accordingly, SNCF looked for an alternative solution in the form of a TGV route which could carry the combined traffic from Montparnasse to the West and from Austerlitz to the South West on a common section of route to a point where the new line could plug into the existing railway network. Detailed studies showed that, by using the infrastructure of an abandoned inter city project from Montparnasse to Chartres known as the Gallardon line, there was potential access straight into Montparnasse station in the centre of Paris. Thus, whereas the PSE line starts 29.4 km (18.3 miles) from Paris the Atlantique line starts almost as soon as trains leave Montparnasse station.

The Atlantique line – which is Y-shaped – starts 3 km out of Montparnasse station. Comprising 280 km (174 miles) of route, the line divides into two separate branches at Courtalain – the Western (Brittany) branch to Connerré where it joins the old route to Le Mans and the South West (Aquitaine) branch which joins the route to Bordeaux just outside Tours. There is also a 17 km (11 miles) continuation bypassing the Tours area, rejoining the Bordeaux line at Monts Junction. Distances are 176 km (109 miles) from Bagneux to Connerré and 87 km (54 miles) from Courtalain to Tours. There are two intermediate TGV stations on the Atlantique line – Massy TGV and Vendôme.

Built to serve the western suburbs of Paris, Massy TGV is the first of four such TGV railhead stations planned for the Ile-de-France region. Located in an environmentally sensitive residential area, Massy TGV station (14 km from Montparnasse) is the start of a cut-and-cover tunnel. There are two long platform loops each capable of holding two Atlantique sets; walls separate the loops from the centre running lines so that non-stopping trains can pass through at 200 km/h without aerodynamic disturbance and with the minimum of noise. Continuous cut-and-cover construction is interrupted at the Paris end of the station to accommodate the junction on to the 'Grande Ceinture' line used by cross-country TGVs to the Sud Est (described later). The new TGV station is alongside Massy Palaiseau station on RER Line B and C, and there are connecting bus services and ample car parking. The two-station complex – which is an excellent example of good integrated transport planning – is joined by an overbridge.

Vendôme is located on the Western (Aquitaine) branch 162 km (100 miles) from Paris. Hitherto, the only service to the town was by slow DMUs from Paris Austerlitz to the old station. Provided as a socio-economic benefit to the town, Vendôme TGV station has been part-funded by the local authority.

The characteristics of the Atlantique line are quite different to those of the PSE. Whereas the maximum gradient on the PSE is 3.5% it is only 2.5% on the Atlantique line. While there are no tunnels at all on the PSE route, the Atlantique line has 2,600 metres of double-track and 9,600 metres of single-bore tunnels at Villejust. These tunnels have been built to a wider gauge to minimise aerodynamic pressures. In singlebore tunnels the free space (i.e. the air section) is 45 sq metre which can be used for 200 km/h and 72 sq metre in large singlebore tunnels which can be traversed at 270 km/h. The maximum speed on the Atlantique line is 300 km/h, the operating headway with TVM 300 is four minutes and power supplies are 25 kV ac.

As was the case with the PSE line, the Atlantique line was commissioned for public service in two stages. The Brittany branch – with services between Paris

To provide ample free air space for high-speed running, Atlantique line tunnels are built to larger dimensions than classic lines. This train is entering Vouvray tunnel - length 1946 metres - which was built to pass under the famous vineyards of the same name. Brian Perren

(Montparnasse), Le Mans, Nantes, Le Croisic, Rennes and Quimper opened on 24 September 1989 – and the Aquitaine branch with services to Tours, Bordeaux, Toulouse and the Spanish border on 30 September 1990.

The Atlantique TGV is also a significant commercial success. Although the line is comparatively short, the train service network covers 2,380 km (1,479 miles) serving 45 towns and cities. In 1991 over 19 million persons used the Atlantique TGV; average daily use is 52,000 passengers with an occupancy rate of 66%. Between 28 October and 3 November 1991, a record 400,000 passengers were carried on the line. Total investment was FFr 18.6 billion at 1990 values The financial rate of return is 12% and the socio-economic figure is 23%. For this project, the French Government made a capital grant of 30% towards the cost of construction.

TGV Nord Europe

The case for TGV Nord – subsequently retitled TGV Nord Europe – which was marginally more robust than that for the Atlantique line, was based on traffic from three sources: domestic travel between Paris and Northern France (the Pas-de-Calais and Nord regions), international traffic from Paris/Brussels to Britain through the Channel Tunnel, and international traffic on the Paris-Brussels-Cologne (Köln)-Amsterdam (PBKA) axis.

Although French domestic traffic between the Nord-Pas-de-Calais region and Ile-de-France region is expected to rise from its present flow of 4.3 million passengers per year to 6.1 million per year by 1997, a significant proportion of the total traffic throughput will be international. This will be more than 22 million a year by 1997. In fact Nord Europe – which was approved in October 1987 – was conceived as an international project in collaboration with the Belgian, German and Netherlands governments; British involvement is through the Eurotunnel fixed link. In this regard BR (European Passenger Services and Railfreight Distribution) and SNCF have acquired 50% of the Channel Tunnel capacity on a long-term contract. Nord Europe is an essential add-on to the Channel Tunnel enterprise – for the London–Paris Eurostar service is only viable with a 3 hour journey time, and this can only be achieved with a 300 km/h railway between the French tunnel portal and the outskirts of Paris Nord.

Paris to Arras opened on 23 May 1993 and Arras to Lille and Calais (Fréthun and the Tunnel Portal) a few months later in September 1993. At the time of writing it is expected that the Channel Tunnel will open in May 1994, but because of production delays with the TMSTs the London-Paris/Brussels service is expected to start in the summer of 1994.

Totalling 333 km (207 miles) of route, Nord Europe starts at Gonesse 16 km (10 miles) out of Paris Nord terminal station. After the junction with the Interconnexion TGV (La Jonction) at Vémars (see below), the alignment is through open country until a point near Estrées-St-Denis from where it shares the same alignment alongside or close to the A1 Autoroute du Nord for the ensuing 85 or so km (53 miles) to the outskirts of Arras. There is a junction at Arras leading to the existing Paris–Lille main line. This will be used by domestic TGVs to Arras, Lens, Béthune and Dunkerque, and to Douai and Valenciennes.

Beyond Arras the TGV line parts company with the autoroute and heads east to Fretin where the line divides into two separate branches – the 113 km (70 miles) line of route through Lille to the French tunnel portal at Fréthun (Calais) and the shorter 12 km (7.5 miles) branch to the Belgian Frontier. This section of the route will not now be completed until 1996.

There are a large number of bridges and viaducts on the route, but no tunnels in open country. Part of the project will include major works in the centre of Lille where the railway will serve a major sub-surface international station complex, the approaches to which will be in cut-and-cover tunnels. Lille Europe station will be located on an inter-link road 450 metres from the existing SNCF Lille Flandres station; the two stations will be served by an extension of the VAL Métro. Not only will Lille Europe station be a major asset for this large and important conurbation, but it will also be used as an international interchange station for passengers from Britain and Belgium to other parts of France.

There will be two other stations in addition to Lille Europe. A station to serve Picardy region (Gare Picarde), which is reasonably close to the town of Amiens whose residents were keenly disappointed that they were not on the direct line of the Nord Europe route, will be located about 125 km (78 miles) from Paris Nord. The second station is at Fréthun (Calais), close to the Eurotunnel complex.

The profile of Nord Europe is designed for a potential speed of 350 km/h (218 mph), but for the present the maximum line speed will be 300 km/h.

TGV Belge

Despite its importance as a key piece of the European high-speed rail network, the first section of TGV Belge will not now open for public service until 1996, with final completion 1998. The delay to this important project – which will be the access for trains from Paris, other parts of France through La Jonction, and from London and other parts of Britain through the Channel Tunnel to Brussels and on to Amsterdam and Cologne – has its roots in the on-going rivalry between the Walloon and Flemish factions of Belgian society.

Plans for TGV Belge were first tabled in 1985 when the decision to build the Channel Tunnel was made. At the end of 1988, the transport ministers of the countries concerned with the European high-speed rail network agreed that 15 May 1993 would be the target date for the completion of the associated infrastructure in France and Belgium. A route acceptable to both the Walloons and the Flemish was finally agreed in July 1991, and the entire project will not now be completed until 1998.

TGV Belge is Y-shaped. The stem of the Y is the interface with SNCF's TGV Nord at the Franco-Belge frontier some 11 km (6.2 miles) to the east of the triangular junction at Fretin. The three sides of the Fretin triangle will provide the following routeings – from the Paris direction to Lille Europe, Fréthun, Calais and the Channel Tunnel; from Paris to Brussels and beyond; and from Brussels to Lille Europe, Calais and the Channel Tunnel. There is no frontier post and as the tracks cross the border TGV Nord Europe becomes TGV Belge.

On the Belgian side of the border the alignment is to the south of Tournai, crossing the River Escaut in Antoing where there is a junction connecting with the existing SNCB tracks from Mouscron to Mons, Charleroi and Liège. Continuing, the route passes two listed sites at Crevecoeur on a viaduct, passes to the south of Ath to cross the River Dendre from where it runs for 11.5 km (7 miles) alongside the existing Tournai-Brussels line as far as Silly. From there the route follows the southern side of the A8 autoroute for 9 km as far as Enghien diverging at Tubize to reach Lembeek. The distance from the frontier to Lembeek is 71 km (44 miles).

From Lembeek the TGV tracks are alongside the existing Mons to Brussels line through Hal and Lot. There will be four tracks from Lot to Brussels Midi – two for classic trains and two for TGVs. All four tracks will enter a new tunnel to reach Brussels Midi station. These works entail about 71 km (44 miles) of new infrastructure out of a total distance of 88 km (55 miles) from the border to Brussels Midi. The line speed will be 300 km/h from the border to Lembeek and 200 km/h from there to the approaches to Brussels Midi.

Beyond Brussels the TGV line will divide into two separate branches forming the two prongs of the Y. The north fork will be the existing route to Antwerp and the Netherlands border at Roosendaal, but upgraded and vastly improved although limited to a maximum speed of 160 km/h.

Antwerp Central station – which is a dead-end terminal – and its associated track layout will be transformed. A new sub-surface station for TGVs and other international trains will be built. The capacity of Antwerp Central station – considered to be the constraining bottleneck of the entire SNCB system – will be doubled. Having considered a number of alternatives, it has now been decided to use the existing classic route through to Roosendaal. This section of line – 76 km (47 miles) – is quite flat and suitable for upgrading to 160 km/h but the track will have to be lifted by specially constructed embankments to eliminate level crossings. Apart from 3 km of new tunnelling at Antwerp, the entire 76 km of route from Brussels Midi to Roosendaal is without tunnels. This work is targeted for completion by the end of the decade.

The other fork of the Y is the route to the east of Brussels through Louvain to Liège and the German border at Aix-La-Chapelle (Aachen). As this route also serves Brussels International Airport (Zaventem), an extra (fourth) track will be added to the existing 7 km of route between Schaerbeek and Zaventem. From Zaventem to Louvain (20 km) there will be two new tracks adding extra capacity and allowing a speed of 200 km/h, while the entry into Louvain station will be eased out to raise speeds from 90 to 160 km/h.

Beyond Louvain new high-speed infrastructure will be built alongside the A40 autoroute allowing trains to run at the full 300 km/h as far as Bierset just before Liège where TGVs will rejoin classic tracks. Beyond Liège there will be new infrastructure including a 7 km single-bore tunnel. After that the new route will follow the southern side of the Liège to Aix-La-Chapelle motorway, on an undulating course which will necessitate the building of several large viaducts. At Welkenraedt, the last station in Belgium before the German border, the TGV will rejoin the existing lines. From Brussels to the German border, 89 km of entirely new infrastructure is to be built – 60% of the total distance of 146 km (91 miles). Given the international character of the section from Liège into Germany, and the increased construction because of the numerous environmental constraints, SNCB is looking to international help from the EC to finance this venture. Target date for the Brussels–German Frontier section is 1998.

La Jonction en Ile-de-France: Paris Interconnexion

Because of its geography and distribution of population, most major road and rail links in France have tended to radiate from Paris. Over two-thirds of journeys by all transport modes are made from province-to-province. Cross-country rail journeys are often slow and in most cases it is quicker to travel via Paris, even though it may entail changing terminal stations. It is for these reasons that rail's market share of the cross-country market is derisory. Nonetheless, as business on the Paris–Lyon TGV service began to grow, research showed that significant numbers of passengers who had joined trains at the Gare-de-Lyon in Paris had started their journeys from places as far away as Lille. There was also significant business from Rouen and the western suburbs of Paris such as Mantes-la-Jolie and Versailles.

To develop this traffic SNCF launched a direct TGV service from Lille to Lyon which bypassed Paris altogether by using a series of freight lines to the east of the city known as the 'Grande Ceinture'. Introduced in September 1984, the Lille to Lyon TGV soon built up custom to the extent that a second service was added plus a similar service to Rouen which also serves Mantes-la-Jolie and Versailles. Today over 500,000 passengers per year use these trains to avoid Paris and obviate the change of terminal stations.

Given the substantial journey time reductions which TGV can offer it is clear that, providing a means of linking the main TGV routes out of Paris could be organised, competitive journey times between the major French centres could be substantially reduced to levels within – or close to – the 3 hours threshold at which point air starts to become more attractive than rail. So far as leisure travel is concerned the times by cross-country TGVs would be far quicker than could ever be achieved by private car. To develop the tremendous potential for cross-country travel by TGV, a new route – known as La Jonction Est – has been developed in parallel with the Nord Europe project. There is also the European dimension – for passengers from Eurostar, TGV Belge and the PBKA axis will be able to get direct to the rest of France. It is an essential part of the European high-speed network.

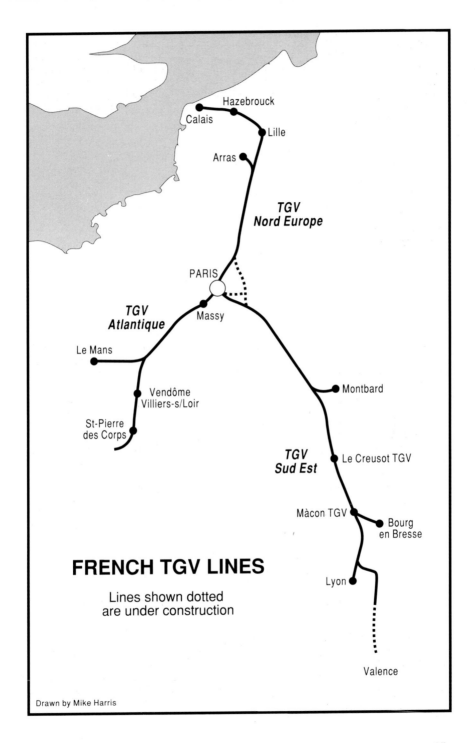

Hazebrouck
Calais
Lille
Arras

**TGV
Nord Europe**

PARIS

**TGV
Atlantique**

Massy

Le Mans

Vendôme
Villiers-s/Loir

St-Pierre
des Corps

Montbard

**TGV
Sud Est**

Le Creusot TGV

Màcon TGV

Bourg
en Bresse

FRENCH TGV LINES

Lines shown dotted
are under construction

Lyon

Valence

Drawn by Mike Harris

Initially this line will provide a link between the Nord Europe line at Gonesse, the PSE line at Moisenay, the Grande Ceinture line at Valenton and the classic route into the Gare-de-Lyon at a point north of Villeneuve-St-George. As can be seen from the map on the previous page, La Jonction is also an extension of the PSE line which will enable trains from Lyon to rejoin the classic tracks into the Gare-de-Lyon about 10 km from the terminus instead of the existing junction at Lieusaint, 29 km from the terminus. As La Jonction line speeds will be in the 200-270 km/h range instead of the low speeds on the existing classic tracks in from Lieusaint, journey times for PSE trains will be reduced by several minutes. For the present, access to the Atlantique line will be through the existing Grande Ceinture tracks from Valenton to Massy TGV station described earlier. Two further connections are being studied – a junction with the proposed TGV Est and a new link (La Jonction Sud) through Melun-Senart, to the Atlantique line. No firm dates have been given for these projects.

Comprising 102 km (63 miles) of route, La Jonction (interconnexion) starts on a triangular junction with the Nord Europe line at Vémars from where it heads south to the Triangle de Coubert (54 km from the start) formed by the junction with PSE northward extension mentioned earlier. The line ends at Moisenay (69 km from Vémars) where it joins the existing PSE tracks about 17 km from the start of the PSE line at Lieusaint. Line speeds will be 200/220/270 km/h.

Another important reason for La Jonction Est – improvement of access for the growing number of people now living in the expanding Ile-de-France region. Increasing numbers of centres of activity such as business and large schools are being built outside Paris and located near good trunk roads. Massy in the west, Marne-la-Vallée in the east and Roissy are becoming large centres of activity, and others are planned. All of these centres need good rail access. The RER (Réseau Express Regional) Paris outer-urban rapid transit system has already been extended into these areas.

Four TGV railhead stations are planned in the Ile-de-France outside Paris. As well as Massy TGV described earlier, similar railheads are planned at Roissy, Marne-la-Vallée-Chessy (for EuroDisneyland) and – although this has not yet been finalised – at Melun-Senart. Situated 7.5 km from Vémars, Roissy is being built to serve Paris (Charles de Gaulle) International Airport. The station, which will have four loop platforms plus two through lines, will access the airport terminals plus RER B which is being extended from its present somewhat unsatisfactory terminus to the new station. Roissy will open in 1994; by 1996/97 2.5 million passengers per year are expected to use the station. Marne-La-Vallée-Chessy (EuroDisneyland) – 31 km (19 miles) from Vémars – will provide an interchange with the existing terminus of RER A. Traffic potential is good. SNCF is estimating 940,000 passengers per year plus more when TGV Est opens on top of which there will be the vast potential from EuroDisneyland who are expecting about four million TGV passengers a year from all over Europe. There will be two platforms served by three tracks, plus two through lines, and TGV stabling sidings at the station. SNCF is considering running special TGV excursion trains to EuroDisneyland station.

Melun Senart is still at the planning stage. Its go-ahead could follow a decision to build the 49 km (30 miles) Jonction Sud. Journey time from Melun Senart will be 2 hours 25 minutes to Nantes and 1 hour 50 minutes to Lyon.

La Jonction Est will cost FFr 11 billion at 1989 values; most of it has been funded by SNCF and a contribution to the cost of Roissy station has been made by the Aeroports de Paris and by the Disney Company towards Marne-la-Vallée-Chessy. The project will be commissioned in two stages – Vémars to Moisenay including Roissy Charles De Gaulle and Marne-la-Vallée-Chessy in late 1994 and Coubert to Créteil in 1996.

Rhône Alpes: the Lyon Contournement

Under the SNCF master plan the PSE line will be progressively extended to serve the Rhône Valley, Marseille, Nice and the Spanish Border. The work, which will take several years to complete, is two projects – TGV Rhône Alpes and TGV Méditerranée. The first stage of Rhône Alpes – also referred to as the Lyon Contournement – from Montanay to St-Quentin-Fallavier, opened on 13 December 1992; the second stage through to Valence will open in May 1994.

While the long-term objective is to serve the entire South of France area, the Rhône Alpes project will bring major benefits in the short term. It will: ease pressure on the existing line capacity in the Lyon area which is reaching saturation, provide a station at Lyon International Airport (Satolas) and it will greatly improve access to the French Alpes. The project – which totals 121 km (75.2 miles) of route – will run to the east of the Lyon conurbation and will start near Montanay just before the existing line ends at Sathonay. From here it will follow an east/south east alignment to Satolas Airport, after which there is a major junction at St Quentin-Fallavier which will give access to the existing line from Lyon to Chambéry and Grenoble. From St-Quentin-Fallavier the route heads south to join the classic PLM line just north of Valence. When this is complete there will be substantially reduced journey times between Paris, Valence and the Rhône Valley and more modest savings to Chambéry and Grenoble.

Line speed will be 300 km/h over most of the route from Montanay to St-Quentin-Fallavier, but because of curvature, tunnels and gradients line speed will be 270 km/h on the southern section. Power supplies will be 25 kV. The southern section of the line will be equipped with TVM 430; headways will be four minutes.

SNCF: HIGH SPEED RAIL ROUTES (Lignes à Grande Vitesse)								
Project	Location	Length of route		Commissioning date	Costs (1990 values)		Rate of return	
		Km	Miles		FFr millions	£ millions	SNCF corporate	Socio-economic
Paris-Sud Est (TGV-PSE)	Lieusaint-Sathonay/ Aisy	417	259.1	First stage: September 1981 Second stage: September 1983	9798	980	15%	30%
Atlantique (TGV-A)	Paris (Bagneux)- Connerré	176.0	109.0	September 1989	10005	1000	12%	23%
	Courtalain-Tours	87.0	54.0	September 1990				
	Tours avoiding line	17.0	11.0	September 1990				
		280.0	174.0					
Rhône Alpes Lyon Contournement	Montanay-Satolas Airport (Lyon) Satolas-St Quentin-Fallavier	138.0	23.6	13 December 1992	6072	607	9%	14%
	St Quentin Fallavier- St Marcel-Valence	83.0	51.6	May 1994				
TGV Nord Europe	Gonesse-Belgian frontier	209.2	130.0	First stage: Gonesse to Arras 23 May 1993 Second stage: Arras to Lille/Fréthun September 1993	13386	1334	13%	20%
	Spur to Arras	10.7	6.6					
	Fretin (Lille)-Fréthun (Calais Channel Tunnel Portal)	113.2	70.3					
		333.1	206.9					
Le Jonction (Interconnexion)	Vémars-Roissy-Airport-Moisenay	102.0	63.4	1994	8004	800	14%	22%
	Coubert-Valenton			1996				
	Total route Km/miles	1253.1	778.6	Total costs	47265	4721		

Single unit Atlantique set at speed. SNCF

2. The Trains:
Trains à Grande Vitesse

At an early stage in TGV development, gas turbine propulsion was seriously considered as the choice of traction. Although on the face of things electricity was the obvious means of powering the new trains, there were lingering doubts about the efficiency of current collection from the overhead catenary at very high speeds. Towards the end of the 1960s the aerospace industry had developed a number of lightweight gas turbines which could offer the same power output over a conventional diesel engine, but at a third of the weight and three-quarters of its bulk. Another significant advantage of gas-turbine engines was economical consumption of low-grade fuel. These new engines seemed ideal for high-speed lightweight trains, and could run at speeds comparable to those offered by electric traction and without the cost of installing catenary. To determine the potential of gas turbine traction in the railway field, SNCF ordered a production series of four-car gas-turbine multiple units, with a maximum speed of 180 km/h (112 mph). These were followed by a second higher-powered series and in 1970 by two experimental sets with a 300 km/h (186 mph) speed.

The Arab-Israeli War in October 1973 made an immediate impact on the security of supply but also on the price of petroleum products, drastically changing the economics of gas-turbine technology for rail traction. Consequently, SNCF undertook more research into the problems of current collection at very high speeds when dual-voltage locomotive CC 21001 was tested at speeds up to 283 km/h (167 mph) in ac mode between Strasbourg and Mulhouse in Alsace. Further study of the issues – and the decision of the French Government to build a national network of nuclear-powered electricity generating stations – led SNCF to opt for electric traction for its TGV project. A high-speed gas-turbine set was built and together with a single unit electric car, was used as a test-bed for the development of the new generation of TGV trains.

The PSE fleet is in the process of being refurbished; this is the upgraded Second Class accommodation. SNCF

Paris Sud Est (PSE) Fleet
An order for two pre-production and 85 production sets (subsequently increased in number) for the Paris Sud Est line was placed with Alsthom (now GEC Alsthom) when civil engineering work on the new line started at the end of 1976.

Four basic design rules were set for the PSE trains and have been perpetuated for all subsequent builds. They are: maximum 17-tonne axle-load; fixed-formation trainsets; articulated configuration for the passenger coaches and body rather than bogie-mounted traction motors.

Each PSE set consists of two power cars enclosed by a rake of eight articulated trailers. Articulation was chosen to permit low-slung bodies to be carried on nine rather than 16 bogies thereby saving weight, minimising energy consumption and enhancing passenger comfort by obviating the need for seats to be installed over the bogies. It is also easier to gain access to low-slung vehicles. With the vehicle ends mounted over the bogies a spacious vestibule area was designed which is tightly sealed to ensure the highest standards of sound insulation and air-conditioning.

When TGVs pass from a 1,5 kV dc to a 25 kV ac area the driver has to lower the dc pantograph, pass through a neutral section, and then raise the ac pantograph. This manoeuvre is indicated at markerboards. The first picture shows the lower pantograph 'baissez panto exécution' board and the second picture shows the point where the 25 kV power supply begins. Brian Perren

To provide sufficient power for sustained high speeds up to 270 km/h and to cope with the 3.5% gradients, to which reference was made earlier, two power cars are provided. There are twelve 535 kW (717 hp) traction motors mounted on six motor bogies, two of which are located under the outer end of the adjoining trailer vehicles R1 and R8. Because significant sections of the SNCF network are electrified at 1.5 kV dc and the cost of converting to the more efficient 25 kV ac is not a practical proposition, the TGV – like most contemporary SNCF locomotives and power cars – is equipped for dual-voltage operation. When operating in ac mode a single pantograph is used for current collection; power to supply the other traction motors at the opposite end of the rake is carried along a 25 kV line along the roof of each unit. In dc mode two separate dc pantographs are used with power supplied direct to the traction motors. The weight of each power car is 64.2 tonnes and within the 17-tonne axle-load.

There are four different PSE versions. Originally there were 92 standard dual-voltage sets, eight standard two-class sets equipped to work on 15 kV 16⅔ Hz ac power supplies for running over Swiss tracks into Lausanne and Berne and nine sets with all First Class seating. (Power supplies over the 15 km section of route from the French border crossing at La Plaine to Geneva main station are 1.5 kV dc). One standard two-voltage set has been withdrawn following collision damage and another unit (No.88), following extensive use as a test train for synchronous traction motors, has been converted to a three-voltage set and renumbered 118. PSE fleet totals are now: nine First Class, 90 two-class two-current and nine three-current 'Swiss' sets, a total of 108 sets. In addition there are the 2½ sets built for the French Post Office service between Paris Charolais, Mâcon, and Lyon postal depots. Designed to carry sacks of mail in containers, the rakes consist of two four-car half-sets instead of the eight vehicle passenger format. This enables a half-set rather than a full eight-car set to provide maintenance cover. From time-to-time, the spare postal power car has been used to deputise for unavailable ordinary two-voltage power cars. These half-sets are permitted to run on their own at a maximum speed of 160 km/h.

A standard PSE set consists of three First Class, a bar/Second Class, and four Second Class vehicles. Each rake is identified as follows: M1 (power car), R1, R2, R3, R4, R5, R6, R7, R8 and M2 (power car). M is French for *motrice* or power car and R is for *remorque* or trailer. The three First Class cars are R1, R2 and R3, the bar/Second Class is R4 and the remaining four Second Class cars R5, R6, R7 and R8.

A mixture of unidirectional and face-to-face seating now consists of 108 First and 260 Second Class. A small aircraft-type galley is located in the vestibule over the bogie between vehicles R1 and R2 to provide a service of meals to First Class passengers at their seats. Following extensive in-service experience a programme of internal modifications has been undertaken. The bar space, which was far too small and cramped, has been extended by removing two bays of Second Class seats in R4 and the seating in First Class car R1 has been modified to provide more space for meal service, reducing the total number of seats in the train from 386 to 368. Telephones are also being installed. Baggage stacks are located at the end of each coach; there is a facility for handicapped passengers and toilets are of the latest retention-type. Two sets can be coupled to work in multiple but there is no passenger access between the two units.

The Atlantique Fleet

By the time a firm order was placed with Alsthom in November 1985 to build 95 Atlantique trainsets – subsequently increased by 10 to a total of 105 – SNCF had accumulated four years technical and commercial experience of operating train services at speeds up to 270 km/h with the PSE fleet. In addition to this day-to-day experience, SNCF – in close association with Alsthom – had initiated a number of technical development programmes with particular regard to riding qualities at even higher speeds, traction motor development and the use of microprocessor technology for a range of operating aids.

Highlight of these tests was a new world speed record of 380 km/h (236 mph) – subsequently bettered in 1990 – with PSE set No.16 on 27 September 1981. This research produced two important technical developments – the decision to use SR 10 air-suspension and synchronous traction motors in the Atlantique design. Surprisingly, despite the excellent performance of air-suspension on other contemporary European rolling stock including its own Corail coaches, SNCF opted to heliocoidal springing for the PSE secondary suspension. Following the satisfactory outcome of tests with the SR 10 suspension, SNCF decided to retro-fit the PSE fleet with this feature.

The most important feature of the Atlantique train is the self-commutating three-phase ac synchronous traction motor. Not only does the synchronous (or commutatorless-motor) provide more power per weight and volume than a conventional motor, but its maintenance costs are very much lower. The commutators on the PSE dc traction motors have to be reprofiled every 300,000 or so kilometres (186,420 miles). Whereas a PSE trainset needs 12 535 kW motors to meet its performance specification, the Atlantique train can function with eight similar size synchronous traction motors with an output of 1,100 kW per motor.

With this extra power – but also allowing that the maximum gradients on the Atlantique line are much less demanding than the PSE – it was possible to add two extra trailers as well as to raise the maximum speed to 300 km/h (186 mph). With eight instead of 12 traction motors, only four motor bogies instead of six are required, obviating the need for equipment to be located at the outer end of the trailers (R1 and R8).

Atlantique trailer bogie equipped with SR 10 suspension.
GEC Alsthom

Atlantique motor bogie.
GEC Alsthom

Atlantique driving cab. The on-board computer is on the right of the console.
GEC Alsthom

GEC Alsthom production line at Belfort showing Atlantique sets under construction. Atlantique production was completed in 1992 and the factory is now concentrating on Réseau and Eurostar construction. GEC Alsthom

Semi-compartment seating is used in two First Class coaches in the Atlantique configuration, branded 'Club Duo' or 'Quarto'. SNCF

Atlantique power car assembly at GEC Alsthom's Belfort works. GEC Alsthom

To cope with 300 km/h two other technical features were incorporated into the Atlantique design – new pantographs and braking system. To ensure efficient current collection at 300 km/h on the new line and speeds of up to 220 km/h (136 mph) on those parts of the classic line (Tours to Bordeaux) where dc current has to be taken from old pre World War 2 catenary, a new pantograph – the GPU – was designed. This has a unique large plunger with a second stage which has also been redesigned. The new design has also been used for the dc as well as the ac pantographs; on classic track in dc mode two pantographs are used. The new braking system makes use of high powered non-ventilated disc brakes in combination with a microprocessor controlled anti-skid device.

Equally important is the application of microprocessor systems both on-board the Atlantique train and at maintenance depots and control centres. In the 10 or so years since the PSE train was designed, both the number and sophistication of computers available on the market has made it possible to develop advanced communication technology for rail purposes. It is now possible to use microprocessors for a range of diverse functions including anything from control of wheel slip, brake monitoring, control of air-conditioning, door closing and the provision of on-board passenger information displays.

Known as 'Tornad', the Atlantique computer network is an on-board data system built around inter-related microprocessors positioned throughout the train. The centrepiece is the two computers located in the driver's cab. These control a range of functions including pre-test of equipment prior to departure, the troubleshooting guide which drastically reduces the time for the driver to locate and rectify any malfunction, monitoring of the braking system both prior to departure and on the move and control of the public address system.

Thanks to train-to-shore radio link, the great benefit of 'Tornad' is the ability to transmit data from the train to the shore and vice versa. For example, not only is the driver warned of any equipment malfunction by reference to the VDU on his cab console, but the fault is retained in the unit's maintenance log book in Châtillon Depot. So at the end of each day's working, the depot has a complete list of faults on every unit before it arrives. This enables the depot to plan the workload and organise the replacement of any spare parts which may be necessary. Another feature enables the depot supervisor to switch on the air-conditioning remotely from his office instead of having to go out to the train – clearly a new-era of rail maintenance technology.

While the appearance and outward profile of the Atlantique trains shows a strong family resemblance to its PSE predecessors, the profile on the higher point of the two power cars has been realigned to give a more integrated roof line. To ensure that the trains are seen as second-generation TGVs, the red-orange finish used on the PSEs has been replaced by a new silver-white and blue finish. These new technical improvements reduced current consumption to a significant extent.

While these sophisticated engineering innovations will be of considerable interest to the connoisseurs of rail traction technology, the internal design improvements and new range of on-board amenities are more readily apparent and have been widely welcomed by SNCF's customers. At the time that the PSE trains were designed, SNCF had started to move away from the luxury market as exemplified by equipment built for the 'Mistral' and Paris-Bordeaux TEEs, and had narrowed its focus towards journey-time reductions and standards of quality aimed to meet the needs of a wider market. Also, it was envisaged that most TGV journeys would be within the $2\frac{1}{2}$ to 3 hour journey time band and it was only later – in response to its customers' wishes – that longer journeys such as 7 hours between Paris and Nice were added to the service. Accordingly, the initial layout of the PSE train is comfortable but relatively simple.

Atlantique Second Class seating. Seats are laid out in pairs each side of the gangway with a mix of unidirectional and face-to-face seating. SNCF

First Class coaches have wider seating and gangway, laid out with single seats on one side. SNCF

With 10 vehicles in the Atlantique formation, it was possible to devote one coach to an attractive bar and lounge area. SNCF

'Espace Jeunes' TGV Atlantique. French Railways

TGV-ATLANTIQUE: TRAIN UNIT FORMATION		
Unit Formation	First Class Seats	Second Class Seats
Power Car No 1 End	-	-
R1 First Class	44	-
R2 First (Club) Class	36	-
R3 First (Club) Class	36	-
R4 Bar	-	-
R5 Second (Coach) Class	-	60
R6 Second (Coach) Class	-	60
R7 Second (Coach) Class	-	60
R8 Second (Coach) Class	-	56
R9 Second (Coach) Class	-	56
R10 Second (Coach) Class	-	77
Power Car No 2 End	-	-
(1) There is also a total of 11 First and 26 Second Class tip-up overflow seats located in vestibules through the train	116	369
	TOTAL: 485	

Partly because average journeys on the Atlantique network are much longer but also because rail has to maintain its competitive edge vis-à-vis other modes of transport, an imaginative range of on-board facilities has been incorporated into the Atlantique design. There are three First Class, six Second Class and a bar/lounge car: a total of 485 seats. The set is numbered M1, R1 to R10, and M2. A welcome improvement is that an entire coach (R4) has been allocated to provide a catering and lounge area, not just as a place to buy drinks and snacks but as a place to linger and socialise; the bar area also includes a shop for the purchase of other items such as magazines and gifts.

As the Atlantique sets only have four motor bogies compared with six in the PSE sets, the space at the outer ends of R1 and R10 is not needed to house an additional motor block and has been used to enhance passenger accommodation. At the First Class end (vehicle R1) the space has been used to create a small but stylish conference saloon with video facilities which can be reserved by businessmen travelling in groups who wish to use the journey time for business meetings. At the opposite end of the rake R10 has been used to provide an Espace Enfants children's play area.

A completely new design concept has been applied to the First Class accommodation. Coach R1, which is next to the power car, is a standard open plan coach with face-to-face seating at tables; there is a facility in this coach for handicapped travellers and their wheelchairs. Seating in R1 is designated 'Coach'.

In the other two First Class coaches – designated 'Club' – the layout is striking and very stylish. On one side of the central aisle the seating is standard open plan with two face-to-face seats and tables; on the opposite side the seating is in groups of four face-to-face with tables but in semi-compartment layout. First Class passengers therefore have the choice of three styles of seating: 'Coach', 'Club' duo or quatro and the *salon*. There is an at-seat meal service supplied from a galley between coaches R1 and R2. All toilets are retention type and there are three telephone cabines in the train.

Seating configuration in Second Class is a mixture of unidirectional and facing. A useful facility has been provided at the adjoining ends of coaches R9 and R8 where the seating has been designed to accommodate families travelling in groups of two to five people; a fifth sideways seat has been fitted between the normal facing pairs of seats. A special nursery toilet is installed over the bogies between the two coaches in the centre of these two family areas.

The Réseau fleet

While the first PSE and second-generation Atlantique trains were designed to meet the characteristics and market needs of these two routes, a new situation will exist from 1994 when the new network of La Jonction inter-réseau cross-country services through the Paris Interconnexion comes into service. To provide inter-réseau services between the Nord, Sud Est and Atlantique lines, and also to provide extra capacity on the PSE line, SNCF placed orders with GEC Alsthom in January 1990 for a build of 80 'Universal' trains designated TGV Réseau (TGV-R). It was originally intended to build 90 Réseau sets, but as the design work was not ready and as both SNCF and GEC Alsthom wanted to maintain the production flow of new trains, the order for Atlantique sets was increased by 10 to 105 and the Réseau build was reduced from 90 to 80. Until sufficient Réseau sets can be assigned to the PSE line on a permanent basis, some Atlantique sets are being deployed on the Sud Est. The first Réseau sets entered service in the spring of 1993; the full build (now 90 again) should be completed by the end of 1994.

Basically the Réseau trains are eight-car versions of the Atlantique trains. They will have eight 1,100 kW synchronous traction motors on four motor bogies providing a total output of 8,800 kW; maximum speed is 300 km/h (186 mph). Their external profile and livery is similar to the Atlantique trains. There are, however, important differences of detail. Because most PSE stations can only accommodate two eight-car sets plus two power cars (totalling 400.38 metres) and as it is not possible to modify such a large number of platforms and station layouts at acceptable cost, the number of trailers has been restricted to eight. Next, so that these sets can work over TGV Belge into Belgium and other SNCB destinations, 30 sets will be equipped to take 3 kV dc power supplies. Thirdly, because of the distance covered by Réseau sets – Brussels to Marseille for example – and as a larger proportion of passengers will be travelling for leisure rather than for business, the internal configuration and seating layouts are different. The formation is similar to the PSE trains, with vehicle designations M1, R1 to R8, and M2.

There will, however, be two versions. Standard Réseau sets have three First Class cars (R1, R2 and R3) with 120 seats, a coach with a bar and some Second Class seats (R4) and four Second Class trailers (R5, R6, R7 and R8) 257 seats: total seating is 377. First Class seating is conventional 'Coach' type with a mixture of unidirectional and face-to-face seating; meal service is from a galley located between coaches R1 and R2. So far as Second Class is concerned, the seats will be reclinable and the pitch has been lengthened; a family area has also been provided. The bar area is about the same as the modified bar on the PSE trains. A modified version – for use on services where there is a higher proportion of Second Class passengers – is being developed. This would have only two instead of three First Class cars and an additional Second Class car; seating capacity would be raised from 377 to 394 places. As on the Atlantique sets, full use has been made of the space – used to house the electrical equipment for the extra motor bogie on the PSE sets under coaches R1 and R8 – at the outer end of the rake. This area is being used to provide a 17-seat standard Second Class compartment and a six-seat salon in First Class. Thus, notwithstanding the wider seat spacing the Réseau trains have 377 seats compared with 368 in the PSE.

PBKA : (Paris, Brussels, Cologne (Köln), Amsterdam)

A long-term issue to be resolved is the question of designing compatible trainsets for working throughout the emerging European high-speed network. In the very long-term one hopes that the railways may move towards technical harmony so that traction current supply systems and signalling systems may be reduced to a more manageable number.

Up to the present time, basic TGVs – plus the Eurostar derivative – have been designed with up to three traction current supply systems. This has enabled TGV services to run from France into Britain and Switzerland as well as being able to use the two SNCF systems. When TGV Belge opens, providing the link through Belgium into the Netherlands and Germany, a total of four different current supply systems will be required – 25 kV from Paris to the approaches to Brussels, 3 kV in Belgium, 1.5 kV from the Belgium border into the Netherlands, 25 kV from just beyond Brussels to the German border and 15 kV 16²/₃ Hz in Germany.

Four-voltage power units are not new. The first such train for international working through Europe was the Swiss RABe Eurocity multiple units built in 1961 for the Trans European Express network. Electrical equipment was packed in a six-axle 100-tonne power car in the centre of the unit. Three years later, Alsthom built a six-axle four-voltage, 109-tonne locomotive (CC40101 series) for SNCF through workings between Paris and Brussels/Liège. An identical version of this locomotive (Class 18) was built for SNCB, units of which currently work from Brussels/Liège to Paris and Cologne.

To work the Paris–Brussels–Cologne–Amsterdam services, SNCF, SNCB, the Netherlands railways and German railways have placed an order for joint purchase of 27 high-speed trainsets – with an option for a further 10 – from a consortium led by GEC Alsthom.

Some considerable time elapsed between the invitation to tender and the response by GEC Alsthom and Siemens for these trains. GEC Alsthom's bid was about 20% higher than the price level envisaged by the four railways while Siemens' was even higher. Discussions continued between the railways and the bidders to see if the price could be reduced to an acceptable level.

Rather than go back to the drawing board for a fresh start, the builders were asked to reduce the level of interior fittings in the train. Given these new parameters, GEC Alsthom produced a new version of its train, basically a four-voltage TGV Réseau. As mentioned, a three-voltage Réseau has already been ordered for working into Belgium as part of SNCF's Nord Europe project for services to Brussels. Even so, the modified Réseau design will still be about 50% more than the railways had originally hoped to pay.

As well as a fourth voltage, the driving cab has had to be redesigned to give better vision for left or right hand running, and to accommodate seven different in-cab signalling systems. The driver's position has been moved from the side to the centre of the cab. GEC Alsthom's design was accepted by the four railways and Siemens withdrew from the tender. The Siemens design had an axle-load of 19 tonnes exceeding the 17-tonne axle-load limit specified by SNCF. Of the 27 sets in the initial order, three will be owned by DB, four by Netherlands Railways, 11 by SNCB and nine by SNCF.

Upper right: **In November 1987 SNCF introduced into service a special test vehicle designed to work marshalled in a normal public-service TGV (PSE or Atlantique) set. It is designated VEGV (Voiture D'Essais Grande Vitesse or high-speed test coach) but also known as Mélusine, which is a symbol of power and beauty. The coach is 24.13 metres long compared with a normal TGV vehicle of 18.7 metres. It is designed to be marshalled between the power car and adjoining trailer vehicles in a TGV set. Partly for aesthetic reasons but also to locate an observation post for viewing pantograph performance, the VEGV roof is contoured to match the rest of the set. VEGV is equipped with a wide range of latest electronic equipment for measuring all aspects of technical performance.This shortened Atlantique set is working with the Mélusine test car.** SNCF

Right: **Mélusine test coach plan.** SNCF

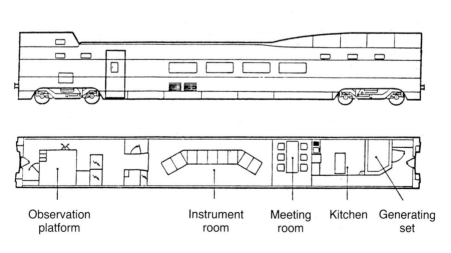

| Observation platform | Instrument room | Meeting room | Kitchen | Generating set |

3. C'Est Possible 515.3 km/h

On 18 May 1990 TGV unit 325 established a new world-speed record of 515.3 km/h (320.2 mph) at KM point 166.8 near the Loir Viaduct between Courtalain and Tours on the South Western (Aquitaine) branch of the Atlantique line. A special test train – which was driven by Michel Massinon – consisted of two power cars and three trailers; totalling 258.8 tonnes and 106.6 metres.

Breaking the world speed record yet again was a major publicity coup for SNCF, but these tests had a far more serious purpose. For a number of years SNCF engineers and technicians, in collaboration with their partners in the railway industry, have been involved in the long-term on-going programme of research for the development of knowledge of high-speed TGV operations and constraints posed by speeds even higher than 400 km/h (249 mph). 270 km/h (168 mph) has been a routine feature of the PSE route since 1981 and 300 km/h is the operating norm for the Atlantique line which opened in September 1989. While these speeds are now a routine feature of French rail travel, they are well below the upper limit of TGV potential. But if higher speeds are to be achieved a wider knowledge of track geometry, current collection, bogie performance and train design and their complex behaviour patterns at higher speeds is essential.

This new record was the culmination of a series of tests which started in December 1989 on the South Western branch of the new Atlantique line before it opened for public service in September 1990. Some 100 safety and research parameters were tested, as were all aspects of passenger comfort.

The parameters determining correct bogie performance were monitored by two types of measurement to evaluate the 'transverse-vertical' force or derailing criteria and overall transverse force or the risk of track shifting.

A most important aspect of the tests was the exploration of the limits of the contact between the pantograph and the overhead power line. The pantograph pushes the overhead line up and this vertical pressure – which occurs as the train moves forward – creates a current wave along the conductor wire. Wave propagation speed is a function of overhead line voltage and is usually around 280 to 310 mph and normally higher than the speed of the train itself. This is the 'critical speed' phenomenon or 'overhead line barrier', which is similar to the sound barrier for aircraft. The tension of the catenary was increased so that the wave speed remained higher than that of the train.

The resonance and oscillation phenomena of the engineering structure decks was analysed on the ground. These measurements were used to determine the effects of noise and vibration along the track and on rail installations, especially on switches and overhead line behaviour and on signalling device and safety installation efficiency. Movement and aerodynamics noise trends in the TGV line area environment were also measured.

Opposite: **C'Est Possible 515.3 km/h (320.2 mph) - the world record run by unit 325.** SNCF

4. Cab Signalling: TVM 430

When the Paris Sud Est line was being planned the performance specification for the route was a two-hour journey time between Paris and Lyon (Part-Dieu), with a five-minute headway and maximum speed of 270 km/h, although the line was designed for an eventual maximum speed of 300 km/h. In the late 1970s these parameters were well ahead of anything previously set for conventional railways in Europe.

Following the commercial success of TGV, which has generated significant new levels of rail travel and has paved the way for other new lines (Atlantique, Nord Europe, Rhône Alpes, La Jonction) to be built, the position has now been reached where capacity must be increased to cope with the volume of business on offer. To remain competitive, speeds must also increase so that journey times can be further reduced. It is for this reason that TGV Nord Europe is being equipped with a new cab-signalling system – TVM 430 – which will allow a three-minute headway between trains running at a maximum speed of 300 km/h.

Signalling is the means of communication between operating personnel on the ground and train drivers, the basic purpose of which is the organisation of train movements in a safe and efficient manner. There are three main functions – correct routeing of trains to avoid conflict with other train movements at stations and other places where tracks merge; the spacing out of trains travelling in the same direction on the same track so that they can stop within a safe distance behind the preceding train; and the prevention of trains travelling in the opposite direction on the same track, although this is normally a problem associated with single-track routes or areas signalled for two-way (bidirectional) working.

PSE driving cabs are equipped with TVM 300 which operates in conjunction with the lineside markerboards located along the high-speed line at driver's eye level. SNCF

It is a tribute to those engineers who pioneered the development of railway signalling that rail is the safest of all transport modes. Hitherto railway signalling has been based on the simple concept of lateral – i.e. trackside – signals which tell the driver the state of the line ahead. Practice varies from country to country, but three aspects are in common use: red for stop, green for safe to proceed, and yellow to warn that the next signal is red giving advance warning to slow down and stop. While these basic principles – supported by audible warning systems in driving cabs – are perfectly satisfactory for speeds up to 200-220 km/h on classic routes a more advanced system is required for trains running at TGV speeds. Visual reaction to lineside signals is no longer a practical possibility at 270 km/h let alone 300 km/h or even higher. A TGV travelling at 300 km/h covers one mile in just 20 seconds.

TVM 300

Having regard to the circumstances posed by these new levels of speed, SNCF decided to introduce a new system of cab-signalling – TVM 300 – on the Paris-Sud Est line. TVM is a French acronym for *Transmission Voie Machine*: i.e. track-to-train transmission.

TVM 300 works as follows. As with all signalling systems – cab or lateral – the first factor to be determined is the distance required for the train to come from its maximum permitted speed to a complete stop. Using full emergency braking, a TGV travelling at 270 km/h needs 3 km (1.9 miles) of level track to stop. In day-to-day service conditions less-severe braking is needed and it may only be necessary for the train to reduce its speed and not stop altogether. Theoretical stopping distances are 6,300 metres (4 miles) from 270 km/h on the Sud Est and 8,000 metres from 300 km/h on the Atlantique line.

To facilitate the braking of the train, but also to reduce the headway between successive trains and consequently increase the capacity of the route, these theoretical stopping distances have been divided into three or four parts, each constituting a 'block section' in signalling terms. Progress from block-to-block is determined by track circuits which monitor the state of the line ahead. The state of these track circuits is picked up from the rails by a receiver on the underside of the power car and decoded through an on-board microprocessor. This data is then used to advise the driver the target speed at which he must enter the next block section. Block sections – or section reference – are indicated by trackside marker boards positioned at driver's eye level throughout TGV routes. The target speed is shown on a digital display on the driver's console.

The displays are:
◆ maximum speed allowed at the next reference point (markerboard) VL (vitesse limité or line speed limit) or 300 km/h, represented by black characters on a green background,
◆ an indication to reduce speed before the next reference point, either because the line ahead is occupied by another train or the train is approaching a junction or diversion location with a lower speed limit; this is represented by white characters on a black background,
◆ an indication – 000 – ordering the driver to stop at the next reference; this is represented by black characters on a red background

Although TVM is based on absolute safety, it is still considered desirable for the driver to retain manual control of the train at all times. There is, however, a fail-safe back-up system. When restrictive information is picked up, advising the driver that he *may* have to reduce speed at the next markerboard reference point, an audible warning is given (horn). If for any reason – possibly because he is incapacitated – the driver fails to respond, the applicable speed is imposed by the fail-safe protection system. Thus, the driver can control the train with due regard to the characteristics of the line (curvature, gradients etc), effective braking and energy-conservation. Indeed, in 12 years experience there have been no untoward incidents on TGV lines.

Given the desirability of retaining manual driving control, it is still necessary to give drivers the maximum possible warning of the state of the line ahead. With classic lineside signalling this is provided by a 'distant' or equivalent signal (double-yellow display on BR), but this is not practical on TGV. Instead, an additional item – the attention indicator – has been incorporated into the signalling sequence. On the PSE sets the digital display sequence is VL (vitesse limité or proceed at line speed); should it be necessary to warn the driver that he may have to slow down or stop VL is replaced by 270, 270 is replaced by 220, 220 by 160, and 160 by 000 (stop). On the Atlantique line the VL indicator is not used. Instead 300 is the line speed display, but – and this is the important difference – the next restrictive display is 300 *flashing*, followed by 270, 220, 160, 000: stop. As mentioned earlier, more-restrictive information is accompanied by the audible cab-signal.

Data from the rails is present throughout the signal section. However, a more restrictive item of information (for example 220 replaced by 160 km/h) is only activated at the next reference point (markerboard) but a less restrictive item of information (160 replaced by 220 km/h) is activated in mid-section. Such a situation can arise where the train ahead is accelerating away from a speed check and the gap between the two trains has widened. As in classic signalling, the spacing of the block section depends on the profile of the line at a given location. On all TGV lines there are some shorter sections on upward gradients and longer sections on downward gradient; this is necessary to ensure the even flow of traffic.

TVM 430

When TVM 300 was chosen for the PSE line it was state-of-the-art, but things have now moved on. Following research during the past 10 years the system has been developed to a point where 28 continuous pieces of information can be transmitted from the track to the train as opposed to only 18 in TVM 300. This is why TVM 430 has been designed and selected for TGV Nord Europe and the southern section of TGV Rhône Alpes. It has also been chosen by EuroTunnel for the Channel Tunnel; here block sections will be shorter and the maximum speed 160 km/h.

Given the ability to transmit and decode 28 pieces of information, it is now possible to extend the range of data to include indications of distance and profile as well as continuous advice regarding the state of the line ahead. This has made it possible to construct a control curve adjusted to the speed and profile of each block section. Whereas TVM 300 can only accommodate one 'attention indicator' aspect – that is 270 on the Sud Est and the flashing 300 on the Atlantique line – TVM 430 can produce a continuous flow of information in a situation where the line ahead is occupied and blocked by the preceding train.

Thus, if the line ahead is blocked, the TVM 430 digital display will show flashing 300, flashing 270, flashing 230, flashing 170, as it passes through the block sections followed by 000 if the train has to stop. As the driver is receiving earlier advice of restrictive information rather than having to wait for his display to change at the next markerboard reference point, he can defer his brake application and deceleration by a few vital seconds. In other words, if braking is deferred the stopping distance and the space of the trains can be reduced without prejudicing safety. However, the automatic override is set at 10 and 20 km/h above the manual deceleration curve; the margin is higher at the end of the section showing 000.

By a continuous display of 'attention indicators' and consequent impact on braking distances, it is now possible to reduce the length of a block section from 2,000 metres (1.2 miles) to 1,500 (0.9 miles). On the face of things this is a small reduction, but when applied throughout a route such as TGV Nord Europe it gives a headway of three minutes in combination with a maximum speed of 300 km/h.

On the Paris Sud Est line (see table) with TVM 300, block sections of 2,100 metres (1.3 miles), the space between two trains is 13,000 metres (8.0 miles) or 2 minutes 54 seconds running time. With 270 showing on the driver's console, the slow down sequence is 220, 160 and 000 bringing the train to a complete standstill in two block sections (i.e. 4,400 metres or 2.7 miles) to the rear of the train ahead.

As the Atlantique trains have superior braking capability TVM 300 has been installed to cope with 300 km/h and block sections of 2,000 metres (1.2 miles) on this line. Because Atlantique trains are longer the spacing between two trains has been extended out to 14,480 metres (9 miles) but the running time remains 2 minutes 54 seconds. The sequence shown on the driver's console is a flashing attention indicator 300, followed by 270, 220, 160 and 000.

Turning now to TGV Nord Europe and TVM 430 a continuous display of flashing attention indications gives the following sequence: flashing 300, flashing 270, flashing 230, flashing 170 followed by 000. Consequently, the spacing between the two trains – but it also has to be remembered that the train lengths on this line are smaller – is reduced to 10,900 metres (6.8 miles), or 2 minutes 11 seconds running time at 300 km/h on level track.

SNCF has also decided to install TVM 430 on the southern section – St-Quentin-Fallavier to Valence – of the Lyon Contournement. As the gradients are relatively severe and as the latest Réseau sets have the same superior braking capability as the Atlantique sets, traffic flow will be improved if TVM 430 is installed over this section. In this case the maximum line speed – determined by curvature and gradient – is 270 km/h giving a spacing of 10,900 metres (6.8 miles) between trains or 2 minutes 25 seconds running time. Stopping sequence – again a continuous showing of flashing attention indications – is shown in the tables on pages 110 and 111.

MAXIMUM SPEEDS AND MINIMUM DISTANCES								
Signalling Type	Train Type	Maximum Speed	Block Section Length (Metres)	Train length with Two Units (Metres)	Distance Between Two Trains (Metres)	Distance in Time	Timetable Headway	Trains per hour
TVM 300 Sud-Est	PSE	270 km/h	2,100	400	13,000	2m 54s	5 min	12
TVM 300 Atlantique	Atlantique	300 km/h	2,000	480	14,480	2m 54s	4 min	15
TVM 430 Nord Europe	Réseau	300 km/h	1,500	400	10,900	2m 11s	3 min	20
TVM 430 Lyon Contournement	PSE	270 km/h	1,500	400	10,900	2m 25s	4 min	15

TVM 300: modifications

Partly to enable PSE sets to work over the southern section of the Lyon Contournement but also to reduce the headway on the PSE line between Lieusaint and Sathonay from 5 to 4 minutes, two changes are to be made to the TVM 300 equipment on the PSE sets. The first modification is technical; the second is procedural.

In order to achieve a headway of four minutes with a maximum speed of 270 km/h – the maximum permitted on the southern section of the Lyon Contournement because of gradients and curvature – a means has to be found of reconciling the different braking characteristics of PSE sets and Réseau sets both of which will work over this route. The modification to the TVM 300 equipment will be made to 50 or so PSE sets which will 'translate' the TVM 430 data from the track so that these sets can stop in the same distance as a Réseau set equipped with TVM 430.

The procedural modification has two features. As described earlier, the original 'line clear' display on the PSE console consisted of two letters VL (Vitesse Limité) or normal speed for that part of the route; if the line ahead is not clear VL is replaced by 270 and so on. Under the revised procedure, the VL indication is preceded by 270 and the attention indicator is 270 flashing. Both PSE and Atlantique sets will now have a flashing attention indicator. Because, as discussed before, TVM 300 data is restricted to 18 pieces of continuous information, the audible warning horn in the cab will function as a 'attention indicator' for restricted information regarding the state of the line ahead and will operate 10 seconds before the approach to the next markerboard reference point. With earlier indication of restrictive information, a driver can more readily anticipate his braking intentions which in turn will reduce the distance he needs to stop. With reduced braking distances, the overlap between two succeeding trains can be reduced to the extent that one block section overlap can be eliminated. Over the length of the PSE line this can be used to reduce the existing headway from five to four minutes. The total number of trains which can be timetabled over the route in a given hour can therefore be increased from 12 to 15. The revised 'attention indicator' procedure will also enable the trains to be signalled over the PSE line at a revised maximum speed of 300 km/h, but this increase is also dependent on other important factors. These include modification of a number of block sections, particularly on rising gradients, and the strengthening of power supplies. SNCF have no plans at the present time to increase the line speed on the PSE route but it is a long-term objective.

Signalling	Type of Train	Maximum Number Trains/hour	Number of Passengers/ hour	Number of Passengers/ Day	Number of Passengers/ Year (Millions)
TVM 300 Sud-Est	PSE	12	12 x 736 = 8,832	8832 x 2 x 15 x 0.8 x 0.75 = 158,976	158,976 x 365 = 58.03 m
TVM 300 Atlantique	Atlantique	15	15 x 970 = 14,550	14,550 x 2 x 15 x 0.8 x 0.75 = 261,900	261,900 x 365 = 95.59 m
TVM 430	Réseau	20	20 x 752 = 15,040	15,040 x 2 x 15 x 0.8 x 0.75 =270,720	270,720 x 365 = 98.81 m
TVM 430	2N Double-deck	20	20 x 1090 = 21,800	21,800 x 2 x 15 x 0.8 x 0.75 = 392,400	392,400 x 365 = 143.00 m

TGV High-Speed: High Volume

New technology – the combination of TVM 430 and TGV trains composed of vehicles with two decks – has lifted the potential of TGV as a mass travel mode well beyond what was envisaged when the PSE line was planned in the 1970s. As the figures in the table opposite show, the situation has been transformed.

Signalled by TVM 300 for a maximum speed of 270 km/h and a five-minute headway, the PSE line can accommodate 12 trains per hour in one direction of travel, each carrying 736 passengers. Taking 12 trains per hour each with 736 passengers you have 8,832 passengers per hour in one direction of travel. If you then multiply 8,832 by two to cover *both* directions of travel you have an hourly figure of 17,664. Assuming 17,664 per hour over a normal daytime span of 15 hours you have an absolute maximum of 264,960 passengers per day. However, one must take account of day-to-day practicalities – for few trains actually load 100% and 80% is a more realistic average load and in normal circumstances it is only possible to use around 75% of the number of theoretical train paths. So, by taking 80% of 264,960 together with realistic average loading you have 211,968 passengers and by taking 75% of that figure you arrive at 158,976 passengers per day on the Paris Sud Est TGV line. Multiply this figure by 365 and you have a yearly total of 53.08 million passengers.

By applying the same criteria to the Atlantique line (TVM 300) you have 95.59 million passengers per year. Réseau sets fitted with TVM 430 will give you 98.81 million passengers per year. With TGV 2N (double-deck) TVM 430 lifts this figure to an incredible 143 million passengers per year. In 12 or so years the potential of a TGV route has been lifted from 58 to 143 million passengers per year, or an increase of 41%.

Running with pantographs down and without power, this PSE train is passing through the neutral section at Lieusaint prior to joining the classic tracks for the final few miles into the Gare-de-Lyon terminal station at Paris. Brian Perren

5. TGV 2N: Double-Deck

Part of the case for building the PSE and Atlantique lines was the need for extra capacity to cope with the growth of passenger and freight traffic in the longer-term. Since it opened in 1981 traffic on the PSE has grown by 190% and the line is reaching saturation point. A similar situation is foreseen with TGV Nord Europe. TGV is a victim of its own success.

In the core PSE markets – Dijon, Lausanne, Geneva, Lyon – TGV has the largest market share and, as no significant reduction of existing journey times is foreseen for several years, growth is likely to follow normal economic trends. However, as existing TGV lines are progressively extended the places served benefit from further journey time reductions. Two PSE examples make the point. With through TGVs via the Lyon Contournement, Grenoble trains no longer serve Lyon and most of them run non-stop to/from Paris in under three hours. This recent improvement will gain SNCF a bigger share of the market. The second example is Paris–Marseille. When the Rhône Alpes is finished in May 1994, journey times to points south of Valence will be cut by around 30 minutes, so the time from Paris to Marseille will be a little over four hours.

As well as this growth in core PSE business south and east of Lyon, there is also the effect of La Jonction to be considered and the new network of Réseau trains from the Nord Europe and Atlantique lines through to the South East of France. This new business will require extra trains, all of which will have to run over existing PSE tracks between Lieusaint and Montanay. In the previous chapter we showed how signalling headways will be reduced on the PSE from five to four minutes giving a total of 15 instead of 12 train paths per hour.

Viewed against the totality of SNCF's business projections three extra train paths in an hour is a useful improvement. There is also the problem of concentrated demand in the morning and evening peaks and when no additional train paths can be made available. SNCF's next step was to look at the capacity of the train itself. Until the introduction of two-unit Atlantique sets between Nantes/Rennes and Lyon in September 1991 with seats for 970 customers, the largest trainload on the PSE was 736 in a two-unit formation. But the penalty for the additional 234 passengers is a 19% increase in train length from 400.2 to 475.18 metres. This is the nub of the problem. For apart from Lyon Part-Dieu and Perrache stations, the platforms at almost all stations on the Sud Est network south of Lyon are unable to accept trains of this length without a costly and long-term programme of station layout modifications. This is not just a question of extending platforms, but would entail changes to pointwork and signalling. It is an unrealistic option.

Over the years SNCF has used double-deck trains to cope with the sheer volume of peak-hour numbers in the Paris suburban area. Indeed, double-deck EMUs are now in use in Brussels, Amsterdam, Zurich and many other European locations. They are an accepted feature of the European scene. Would the double-deck concept work for TGV? Building a simple, robust double-deck coachbody mounted on conventional bogies to run at a maximum speed of 140-160 km/h is one thing – a double-deck train capable of running at 300 or 350 km/h is quite clearly a horse of a different colour.

Opposite: **Staircase of TGV 2N.** French Railways

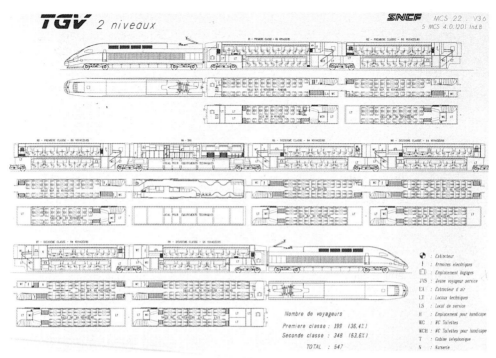

Nombre de voyageurs

Premiere classe : 199 (36,4%)

Seconde classe : 348 (63,6%)

TOTAL : 547

🧯	: Extincteur
⌐	: Armoires électriques
⊡	: Emplacement bagages
JVS	: Jeune voyageur service
EA	: Extincteur d'air
LT	: Locaux techniques
LS	: Local de service
H	: Emplacement pour handicapé
WC	: WC Toilettes
WCH	: WC Toilettes pour handicapé
T	: Cabine téléphonique
N	: Nurserie

TGV 2N: configuration. SNCF

All TGV and TGV derivatives built so far (PSE, Atlantique, TMST, Réseau) have low-slung bodies, articulated bogies and a strict maximum 17-tonne axle-load. Nonetheless, two options were considered – a conventional train with six vehicles mounted on conventional bogies or a classic TGV rake with eight articulated trailers. While the conventional six-coach option would simplify the task of meeting the 17-tonne axle-load constraint, this was the only tangible advantage. In contrast, an articulated configuration has many advantages – in particular better aerodynamics. Not only would there be less resistance to acceleration, but greater ability to eliminate pressure waves at a cost of about 1% of the total price of the train as opposed to 10% for a classic non-articulated version. Above all else, because the floor level of low-slung bodies is lower than the bogie in an articulated set, the space above the bogie which cannot be used for low-level seating can be used to provide the interconnecting vestibule on the upper-deck.

Given equal length, comfort and similar standards of interior décor, an articulated two-deck train will provide 10 to 15% more seats than conventional bogie coaches. It would enable continuous passenger circulation between coaches at the upper-level without loss of space. In all respects, capacity and optimum use of space – the articulated format was the ideal choice, but provided it could be built within the 17-tonne axle-load limit.

By 1987 SNCF's engineers had concluded that a two-level TGV was technically feasible. At that point designer Roger Tallon was brought into the project. Now the only remaining concern was if the choice of a two-deck train – hitherto associated exclusively with high-density suburban travel – would prejudice the high profile image of TGV, so carefully cultivated by SNCF's marketing department. Commercial acceptability also had to be proved. First, a full-size mock-up was built in the Paris Landy workshops so that people could judge the design. At the same time a PSE set was fitted out with the interior décor proposed for the lower deck of the new trains and put into normal public service. At the end of 1988, two vehicles in another PSE set were fitted out so that the kinetic aspects (inertia and position of the centre of gravity) of two-level high-speed stock could be evaluated.

So far all technical and design work had been going forward on the assumption that the train weight would conform to the 17-tonne axle-load. SNCF are adamant that the quality of ride standards set for TGV can only be sustained if track wear and maintenance is minimised, and that such standards are only possible if axle-loads are restricted to an absolute maximum of 17 tonnes. With some Atlantique vehicles already close to these limits, considerable efforts would therefore be necessary to achieve this limit for a taller vehicle carrying 40% more passengers. Three options were considered – the use of steel with a high elastic limit already used successfully to reduce the weight of Atlantique power cars; stainless steel, which obviates the weight of paintwork but needs spot welding which gives less resistance to impact, or aluminium.

As well as giving a structure-weight reduction of 20% compared with 10% for the two other options, aluminium lends itself to the fuselage-image which is characteristic of double-deck trains. Lighter structures are not enough, however, and further work on other parts of the train was undertaken. Some 200 kg has been saved from the mass of the Y 237 bogie used on the Atlantique train which will be retained for the double-deck. Further weight has been saved by using drilled hollow axles in the form of tubes and the pneumatic reservoirs for the secondary suspension have been separated from the structure so that they too can be made from aluminium. The train's internal fittings also provided scope for weight savings – seats, structures, air-conditioning pipes, internal cabling, paint work have all been scrutinised and additional weight savings achieved.

That the complexities of TGV 2N have been translated into a viable, technical and commercial proposition, reflects great credit on the joint SNCF-GEC Alsthom design team and their colleagues at Alusuisse. Early in 1990, the project had been developed to a point where SNCF were able to issue an invitation to tender in March of that year. Three months later GEC Alsthom responded; detailed negotiation of technical and financial details were concluded in February 1991. On 20 June 1991 a firm order for 45 sets with an option for a further 55 sets was placed by SNCF with GEC Alsthom. The first preproduction set should be delivered in the second half of 1994 with delivery of the production sets in the second half of 1995 at the rate of two to three trains per month.

Like the Réseau and PSE sets, the 2N will have eight trailers enclosed between two power cars – but here the similarity ends for the double-deck is in every respect new-generation. Vehicle numbering is the same; coaches are numbered from R1 to R8 and the two power cars are M1 which adjoins coach R1 and M2 which adjoins coach R8.

Access to the train is through large plug doors which lead to a spacious vestibule area and the stairway to the upper deck. In the three First Class coaches (R1, R2 and R3) the stairs are located at the end of the coach next to the catering service car R4, but in Standard Class (coaches R5, R6, R7 and R8) the stairs are at the opposite end of the coach to facilitate access to the bar area. End-to-end access throughout the length of the train is along the upper decks; the accommodation in the lower decks is in self-contained saloons. The upper deck of the catering service car (R4) is used for a spacious bar area and there is a galley for the First Class at-seat meal service; the lower deck is used to house auxiliary equipment. In this regard the air-conditioning load of the 2N is double that of a conventional single-deck train.

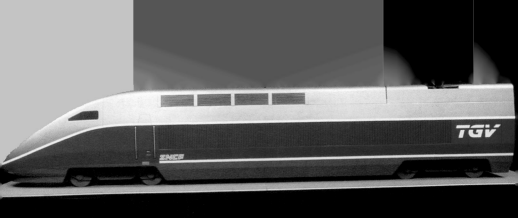

Top: **Side-view artist impression of 2N power car.**

Above left: **Front end of 2N power car.** SNCF

Above: **The driving position on the 2N train has been moved to the centre to give the driver improved visibility.** SNCF

Left: **Prototype double-deck body-shells on test with Atlantique power cars and Mélusine test vehicle.** SNCF

Second Class double-deck saloon. SNCF

Side-view mock-up of TGV 2N exterior. SNCF

The two power cars are a completely new design concept. Modifying the Atlantique power car for the 2N was briefly considered but as this would have entailed redesigning the chassis this option was not pursued. Instead, designer Roger Tallon produced an entirely new format. The power car nose has been redesigned to reduce still further the aerodynamic pressure when trains enter tunnels. A significant development is the new layout in the driving cab, where the driver's position has been moved from the left side to the centre. The reasons for this change are twofold. SNCF envisage using 2N sets to work services into Belgium and Switzerland, plus Germany, the Netherlands and Italy in the longer-term. Not only will cross-border working entail additional items of cab signalling equipment, but placing the driver in the centre of a cab will improve his vision. With the exception of parts of Alsace and in complete contrast to the road network, French trains travel on the left track. Switzerland and Belgium also run on the left, but the Germans, Dutch and Italians drive on the right. A central position will offer good visibility on all neighbouring networks, plus those parts of SNCF where double-track routes have been signalled for two-way working.

The redesigned power car – incorporating the use of high elastic limit steel – has produced a weight saving of about one tonne. This will be used to add a refrigerator, plate-warmer and toilet in the cab area. On some very long driving turns – Paris to Toulon or Paris to Hendaye for example – easy access to a toilet at intermediate stops is very necessary.

A larger structure has also enabled disc-brakes to be used on both sides of motor-bogie wheelsets.

Like all other TGVs power supplies will be 25 kV ac and 1.5 kV dc, but some sets may also be equipped with 3 kV dc for working into Belgium and probably Italy. By adding the fourth European voltage 15 kV 16 2/3 Hz – which SNCF designers say is perfectly possible – the 2N could travel anywhere in Europe. Indeed, if the Union Rail line from the Channel Tunnel through Kent to King's Cross or St Pancras is built to UIC GB+ gauge, the 2N could run through to London, providing it complied with Channel Tunnel safety constraints.

In the same way that the double-deck train has enabled SNCF to substantially increase the number of seats per train – and per train movement – on intensively-worked critical sections of the suburban network out of Paris, the same concept can be applied to sections of TGV route such as Paris–Lyon and Paris–Lille where demand is already high and rising and where track capacity is likely to be an issue in the foreseeable future. Additional line capacity created by TVM 430 in combination with double-deck trains could raise route throughput from 8,832 to 21,800 passengers per hour in each direction – equal to a motorway with six lanes in each direction.

M1 Power car

R1 First Class non-smoking, 67 seats (38 upper, 29 lower deck); 5.5 sq metre baggage compartment, one space for handicapped passenger with wheelchair

R2 First Class non-smoking, 65 (35 upper, 30 lower) seats, telephone, two toilets

R3 First Class smoking, 65 (35 upper, 30 lower deck) seats.

R4 Bar and galley for meal service and conductor's compartment on upper deck; auxiliary equipment lower deck

R5 Second Class smoking, 84 (44 upper, 40 lower) seats, telephone, two toilets

R6 Second Class non-smoking, 84 seats (44 upper, 40 lower); family seating space

R7 Second Class non-smoking, 84 seats (44 upper, 40 lower); family seating space

R8 Second Class non-smoking, 96 (44 upper, 40 lower) seats, two toilets, two compartments for unaccompanied children (12 seats), one baggage compartment

M2 Power car

6. Eurostar: TGV Trans Manche

When the Paris Sud Est TGV was inaugurated few would have envisaged that 13 years later the Channel Tunnel would be open with through high-speed trains from Paris (and Brussels) to London. Eurotunnel's vast £8.1 billion project is almost complete. Tunnelling was completed in June 1991; work is in progress to fit the system with track, signalling, lighting, overhead power supplies etc. There will be four separate services through the Tunnel, all using the same pair of tracks, each of which is in a 50 km (31-mile) single-track bore. They are:

Le Shuttle
These are Eurotunnel's own purpose-built trains which will operate a dedicated service between Folkestone and Calais carrying cars, lorries, motorcycles etc. between its own two self-contained terminals.

International freight trains
A new network of through international freight trains linking a range of destinations in Britain with mainland Europe. These services are organised and marketed by British Rail (Railfreight Distribution), SNCF and – according to the destination/origin in mainland Europe – other European railway administrations.

European Night Services
Due to start in 1995, a service of through overnight trains including both sleeping and seating accommodation between various points in Great Britain and Paris, Brussels, Amsterdam, Cologne (Köln), Dortmund and Frankfurt.

Eurostar
This is the brand name given to the new service of TGV-type trains between Paris Nord/Brussels Midi and London (Waterloo International) starting in 1994. This service will be jointly operated by BR (European Passenger Services), SNCF and SNCB who have purchased a fleet of 38 TGV-type trains generally referred to as Trans Manche Super Trains.

Some important points should be noted. While Eurotunnel is the operator and owner of the Channel Tunnel, 50% of the Tunnel capacity has been leased to BR (European Passenger Services and Railfreight Distribution) and SNCF for the passage of international passenger and freight trains. The agreement between Eurotunnel and BR/SNCF specifies that the journey time between London and Paris must be within a time bracket of 2 hours 55 minutes and 3 hours 10 minutes; at present this schedule can only be achieved by trains running at 300 km/h between the French Tunnel Portal and Paris over dedicated high-speed tracks. Hence TGV Nord Europe.

During the past 30 or so years the traditional rail business between the UK and France and Belgium has dwindled away from its post-war peak, leaving a baseload of under a million journeys by classic rail-ship or catamaran-rail services. This decline is attributable to the growth of the European network of

Above: **This view of the Eurostar power car shows its family resemblance to other TGV builds.** EPS

Eurostar First Class seating. EPS

frequent – but not necessarily cheap – airline services and to the phenomenal growth in cross-Channel car-coach ferry services. Today the classic rail service through Dover and Calais to Paris or through Ostend to Brussels cannot possibly match a 3½ hour centre-to-centre airline time between London and Paris or Brussels for the business traveller. Classic rail travel can no longer match the convenience of using a car for a family holiday in Europe or for budget price destination-to-destination package holiday by coach.

With Eurostar all this will change. The cross-Channel market is significantly larger than it was 30 years ago and its characteristics are now totally different. This is the age of mass travel and expectations are very much higher. Research has identified a very large potential market for through rail journeys via the Channel Tunnel, as well as Eurotunnel's own separate car and lorry shuttle trains.

While a competitive city-to-city journey time, regular frequency, and 20 million seats a year to sell will give Eurostar a sharp competitive edge over its market rivals, these are not enough to ensure success. The service will be keenly priced, aggressively marketed and above all reliable.

Although the trains will run over three national railway systems and over Eurotunnel's tracks, the service – or product – will be homogenous. Staff will be recruited in Britain, France and Belgium and at least half of the passengers will at any time be outside their own country. Rather than each railway working in isolation the three railways – European Passenger Services, SNCF and SNCB – decided to set up a small group known as the Joint Business Management Team. Its terms of reference are to produce and implement a single business and marketing strategy, including pricing policy, branding and advertising, computerised seat reservations system, and the on-board service contract.

By far the greater part of Eurostar's business will be carried on its core service between Waterloo International, Paris Nord or Brussels Midi. Most of the British passengers will live within the London and South East area and unless they reside close to Heathrow or Gatwick airports, are likely to switch to rail for business and leisure travel. There is also an important market in the British regions. With this in mind, Section 40 of the Channel Tunnel Act requires BR to produce and publish plans for passenger services directly to these regions.

For technical reasons the market beyond London is difficult to serve. While the East and West Coast routes are electrified, the Great Western and Midland Main Lines are not. This imposes restrictions on the number of destinations that EPS can serve with a TMST. Even so, plans have been finalised to run Eurostar services from a number of major cities – including Edinburgh, Newcastle, Manchester and Birmingham – to both Paris and Brussels. In the short-term the case for these services is marginal, but long-term prospects are good. The main target market will be leisure travel.

At present there are no plans to run Eurostar trains beyond Paris Nord and Brussels Midi. (There may however be occasional special excursions to Euro Disneyland). The market tends to fragment beyond these two centres and even if the demand is there, the trains would have to be equipped with a fourth or even fifth current collection system. However, the Eurostar service is being planned to give a series of on-going connections at Lille Europe TGV station and at Brussels Midi.

As described in Chapter 1, by 1995-96 with the opening of its La Jonction service through the Paris interconnexion TGV, through TGVs from Lille Europe to Lyon, Marseille, Tours, Bordeaux, Rennes and Nantes will be introduced. These will connect with Eurostar services from the UK. At Brussels Midi, Eurostar will connect with the PBKA service to give competitive journey times through to Cologne and Amsterdam.

Until plans for a new high-speed railway from the Channel Tunnel through Kent to the proposed international terminal station at King's Cross or St Pancras are implemented, hopefully by the year 2000, Eurostar trains will use existing Network SouthEast tracks from Waterloo International to the British Tunnel Portal. To accommodate Eurostar trains – as well as providing capacity for international freight trains and Kent commuters – the two routes via Tonbridge and Maidstone East have been substantially upgraded. The tracks have been strengthened, power supplies increased, new signalling installed and track layouts modified at key locations. This will enable TMSTs to operate at 160 km/h (100 mph) for most of the way between Tonbridge and the Tunnel. A magnificent new station at Waterloo International has been built to handle the new service.

There will be an hourly Eurostar service from Waterloo International to both Paris Nord and Brussels Midi. Some trains will call at Ashford, Fréthun and Lille

Europe. Depending on the number of intermediate stops the journey time will be around 3 hours to Paris and 3 hours 10 minutes to Brussels. Some trains will run non-stop between Waterloo International and Paris Nord and Waterloo International and Brussels Midi. Until TGV Belge opens in 1996, the Brussels trains will run over existing classic tracks at 160 km/h. When TGV Belge opens the journey time between Waterloo International and Brussels Midi will be reduced to about 2 hours 40 minutes.

In 1995 through services from Scotland and the North of England will be added to the timetable. There will be departures from Edinburgh, Manchester and Birmingham to both Paris and Brussels; these will run over the East and West Coast Main Line to the outskirts of London and then over the Network SouthEast lines to the Tunnel.

As the Channel Tunnel project gained momentum BR, SNCF and SNCB set up a working group to produce a jointly-acceptable technical and commercial specification for a train which could run through France and Belgium, pass through the Channel Tunnel and then run over British tracks to London and places in the North of England. Generally referred to as the Trans Manche Super Train (TMST) it will be identified by the Eurostar branding. To develop the design of this train, a working group – known as the International Project Group – began consultations with railway manufacturers who formed a consortium known as the Trans Manche Super Train Group. At the same time a group of designers was engaged to develop the external and internal design of the train. This group is led by GEC Alsthom. An initial contract – which was signed in December 1989 – was for a build of 30 trains. Subsequently, another four sets were added to the basic order followed by a further four sets to cover the north of London services, to make a total of 38 trainsets. Although the fleet will be operated on a joint basis, 18 sets will be owned by EPS, 16 by SNCF and four by SNCB. Seven of the 18 sets will be shortened to run to destinations north of London.

The 31 basic sets consist of a power car, 18 trailers and a second power car; the outer end of each trailer car (R1/18) is also powered from equipment located at the end of the coach which is mounted on a motor bogie. To conform to the safety requirements necessary for the passage of the Channel Tunnel, the complete 2+18 set consists of four detachable elements – two power cars and two sets of nine fixed-formation articulated units. The formation has been designed in this way so that in the event of a failure or emergency while passing through the Channel Tunnel the train can – if circumstances dictate – be uncoupled and each half hauled out of the Tunnel independently. The layout of the two nine-car units which form the complete 18-car set are numbered from R1 to R9 while the companion unit – which is formed in the reverse opposite order – is numbered from R10 to R18. In other words vehicles R1 and R18, R2 and R17 etc are identical.

Because of technical complications, plans to run Eurostar trains to points north of London have taken some time to mature. Partly because of the problems of accommodating a train of almost 400 metres at most British InterCity stations and also so that a greater number of destinations could be served, a plan was devised whereby a basic 2+18 TMST could be divided into two 1+9 half-sets with intermediate driving positions at the end of coaches R9/R10. In the event this was impractical; instead a shortened 2+14 319-metre version of the basic TMST is to be built for these services.

Since two-thirds of the journey between London and Paris will be over TGV Nord Europe tracks, the TMST meets the full basic design rules set by SNCF for its TGV trains. Consequently, they will be fixed-formation articulated units with a 17-tonne axle-load. To provide sufficient power for the 800-tonne formation to run at speeds up to 300 km/h (186 mph), the train is equipped with 12 1,166 kW asynchronous traction motors giving a total output of 14,000 kW or 18,756 hp. Given the need for 12 traction motors and in order to keep axle-loads within the specified 17-tonne limit, there are six motor bogies in each rake. Two bogies are under each of the two power cars, as mentioned, the other two are positioned at the outer end of coaches R9 and R10.

TMSTs will have to work with three different power supply systems – 25 kV ac for SNCF and Eurotunnel, 3 kV dc for SNCB and 750 V dc third-rail for NSE. North of London sets will also use 25 kV on the East and West Coast Main Lines, although these power cars are modified. Each power car will have two pantographs – a standard TGV 25 kV and a special design for Belgian overhead lines. Third-rail shoe gear will be fitted for taking current over Network SouthEast tracks between London and the Tunnel Portal. These will have to retract when the trains enter the Tunnel in order to conform with the Eurotunnel and UIC loading gauge. Unlike the TGV – which only uses one pantograph in ac mode which supplies current to both power cars through a cable along the roof of the train – each TMST power car will be fed by its own pantograph. Power for the motor block in the adjoining outer-end trailers will also be supplied by this pantograph. Given about 400 metres between each power car, the contact wire should be sufficiently stable even at 300 km/h for the second pantograph to make good contact. Voltage changeover – from ac to dc or vice versa – is executed at speed as the train passes through dead sections which are marked by lineside markerboards. A similar procedure will apply at Dollands Moor when passing from third-rail to 25 kV; shoe gear will then have to be retracted or lowered. Voltage changeover is initiated by the driver; a back-up system prevents faulty operation.

The TMST driving cab has a wide range of equipment and is one of the most sophisticated in the world. There is a computer console, 'cruise' speed-control, plus a number of different cab-signalling items. These include TVM 430 for TGV Nord Europe and Eurotunnel; KVB and the 'Crocodile' automatic warning system for SNCF, TBL for SNCB and BR standard AWS with provision for whatever choice of BR automatic train protection system which may be installed later. The driver's position is located at the centre of the cab. The on-board computer system handles a significant number of train operating activities. It links the driver's braking and traction controls with the electronic systems which ensures that the current collection is supplied to the motors in both power cars at the opposite ends of the train. The computers also control the passenger information systems in the train which display the time of departure, destination and so on. In addition, the computers also monitor information for alarm systems.

All passenger areas have air-conditioning. There are two catering service cars (R6 and R13) with a small lounge area, bar, a full kitchen for preparation for meals for First Class passengers at their seats in coaches R7/12, R8/11 and R9/10. Unlike the basic SNCF TGV versions (the PSE, the Atlantique, Réseau, 2N and PBKA) the TMST kitchens will be equipped to either cook food on-board or give an airline-style tray meal service.

There will be facilities for mothers with infants, family areas and two areas dedicated to disabled passengers. Train-to-shore telephones – for universal use in Britain, France and Belgium – will be installed. Baggage compartments with 6.4 square-metres of space for luggage and parcels traffic are provided in R1 and R18 next to the power cars. Each 2+18 set will have 210 First and 584 Standard Class seats – a total of 794; seating layouts will comprise 144 First and 144 Standard face-to-face and 66 First and 440 Standard unidirectional.

The opening of the Channel Tunnel brings international railway operations on a scale well beyond what is currently the case anywhere in the world.

Whereas British aviators, mariners and drivers routinely take their aircraft, ships, coaches and lorries to a range of European destinations, the operational range of British railways has hitherto been constrained by Britain's island status. In 1994 all this will change. Eurostar trains manned by British, French and Belgian crews will run through the Channel Tunnel directly between the three capital cities in some cases without any intermediate stop.

The decision for train crews to work throughout between London and Paris/ Brussels was made on business, operational and productivity grounds. Stopping a Eurostar train en route just to change crews adds needless time to the schedule – there is little purpose at running at 300 km/h (or 3 miles per minute) between Paris and Fréthun and then stopping for a five-minute crew changeover. Another reason for obviating intermediate train crew stops is that it introduces a potential source of unreliability into the operation. If a train from London or Paris is delayed en route, a situation could arise when the driver does not get to the changeover point in time to take over his return working. Then the delay is spread to two trains affecting both directions of travel rather than containing it to one. It also has to be borne in mind that EPS and SNCF have to buy their slot through the Channel Tunnel and failure to arrive at the specified time could generate further problems.

For safety reasons, each TMST will have a minimum crew of five – a driver, two train captains and at least two catering staff. Two catering staff – who will be deployed at the two buffets – is the minimum staffing level, but when full meals are served additional staff will be provided. As well as their basic food-service duties, catering staff will also be required to assist with safety procedures such as detraining and evacuation of passengers from the train in an emergency. Language proficiency in English and French (plus some German and Flemish on trains bound for Brussels) will be required; staff will also be required to pass a stringent test on safety procedures.

Not only is the TMST the most complicated train ever designed, but its drivers will need skills and route knowledge to work on British Rail, Eurotunnel, SNCF and SNCB. This involves detailed knowledge of four different signalling systems, four different sets of rules and procedures and three different types of electric power supplies. Given the quite different skills and know-how needed to drive these new international trains, EPS has created a new position of international driver. Drivers and train captains will be provided by EPS, SNCF and SNCB on a basis agreed through established international railway procedures for the operation of international trains across national borders.

Day-to-day operational supervision of Eurostar trains will be managed from an international operation centre – *Centre De Controle Voyageurs* (CCV) – located at Lille Europe. It will be situated alongside a similar office for international freight traffic through the Channel Tunnel and for SNCF domestic operations. CCV's principal tasks are to implement short-term changes to the basic timetable service, supervise the disposition of the TMST fleet, adjust and restore the service in response to disruptions and collect data for quality improvements. CCV will also monitor the disposition of TMST trainsets against their scheduled work programmes. They will ensure that sufficient trainsets are located at the overnight stabling points to cover the following day's service. In the event of a major disruption to the service, it may be necessary to adjust the maintenance cycles of the train and rearrange the workload between the three depots at London (North Pole), Paris (Le Landy) and Brussels (Forest).

Paris to Geneva TGV at Bellegarde; the Corail push-pull train on the right provides the connecting service to Evian. Brian Perren

7. Paris Sud Est

We described in an earlier chapter how maximum TGV speed has been raised to 300 km/h and how a world-record maximum speed of 515 km/h was achieved. These maximum speeds have tangible publicity value, but SNCF's customers are more concerned with how this technology is transformed into journey times – for it is journey time rather than speed per se that generates customers.

TGV has two main competitors – air for business travellers and the top end of the leisure market such as Paris to Nice, and the family motorcar. Unlike Britain there is no national network of long-distance coaches in France. When the PSE line was being planned, SNCF's target was a 2 hour journey time between Paris and Lyon, compared with 3 hours 45 minutes by conventional train over the old PLM route. Thus, all services to Lyon and beyond were accelerated by at least 1 hour 45 minutes. Because the distance over the new line is shorter, journey time savings to Dijon and beyond was about 40 minutes. Also, with superior acceleration and braking capability, TGVs are able to run at higher speeds on conventional routes where track geometry, curvature and signalling permits. 200 km/h is allowed over certain sections of the Rhône Valley main line between Valence and the northern outskirts of Marseille.

With a journey time of just 2 hours between two centres as important as Paris and Lyon, unless you live very close to both airports air cannot now compete on a centre-to-centre basis. Given the high cost of motoring in France (petrol plus *autoroute* tolls) compared with the reasonable level of fares charged, TGV is an attractive option for the family traveller. As well as being a plausible alternative to air and the car, a large new market has opened up by those who use TGV simply because it is there. You only have to travel by the 0645, 0700 or 0730 from Paris to Lyon to see the large number of businessmen going to Lyon for morning meetings. Having completed a full morning's work, many of these customers return at noon, take lunch on the train, and are back at their desks in Paris for the afternoon. Likewise Lyon businessmen make similar quick visits to Paris.

TGV has also generated a significant increase in travel purely for leisure or social purposes. Many French people – even with comparatively modest incomes – have simple second homes in the country and many have strong family ties in the provinces. Weekend travel for visiting friends and relations is very popular, and a good source of business. For example, Avignon is 408 miles from Paris and the journey time is around 3 hours 45 minutes – but you can leave Paris as late as 2000 and be in Avignon before midnight. You can leave as late as 1900 on Sunday evening or as early as 0502 on Monday morning and be back in time for work on Monday. It is against this business background that we can look at the structure of the TGV service network.

Paris-Lyon
Linking two of France's largest conurbations, the Paris–Lyon service is the core PSE route. There are two main stations in Lyon – Part-Dieu which opened in 1982 and Perrache, the original main station serving the city. All TGVs from Paris terminating at Lyon call firstly at Part-Dieu and then run round to Per-rache; likewise trains originating in Lyon bound for Paris start at Perrache and make a second call at Part-Dieu. The majority of Lyon passengers now alight/join at Part-Dieu. Journey time by the best services between Lyon Part-Dieu and Paris is 2 hours (*vitesse commerciale* 214 km/h: 132.7 mph). The journey time from Part-Dieu round to Perrache takes around 10 minutes. There are 21 basic services in each direction between Paris and Lyon, but there are additional services on Fridays. Basic frequency is around 30 minutes during the morning and evening peak and at most other times there is a train every hour. There is a large proportion of First Class travellers on the route. A through service to the industrial town of St-Etienne is operated as part of the basic Paris to Lyon timetable. There are three services a day in each direction between Paris and St-Etienne and these trains are detached/attached from a Lyon service at Part-Dieu.

From 1985, when the classic line from Lyon to Grenoble and Chambéry was electrified, the TGV service between Paris and Grenoble was also worked as part of the Paris–Lyon service. A major restructuring of the Paris–Grenoble TGV service was introduced on 13 December 1992 when the first (northern) section of the Lyon Contournement was opened. Instead of running through Lyon, Grenoble trains now leave the original PSE line at Montanay from where they will continue at the full 270 km/h line speed as far as St Quentin-Fallavier where they will join the existing line from Lyon to Grenoble; using the new line and avoiding the stop at and slow passage through the Lyon area will save about 20 minutes. This will give a non-stop timing of 2 hours 55 minutes between Paris and Grenoble – within the critical journey-time threshold where rail is more attractive than air on a centre-to-centre basis. There are six services in each direction; when the station is ready some of these trains will serve Lyon Satolas Airport.

A completely new station was created at Lyon Part-Dieu for the launch of the Sud Est TGV network. This attractive arcade has a restaurant, cafe, shops and information facilities for passengers. SNCF

The Gare-de-Lyon station throat was substantially modified to provide access to additional platforms for the increased business generated by TGV. Brian Perren

The sales and reservation centre at Paris Gare-de-Lyon station.

Rhône Valley, Montpellier, Marseille

Most of the TGVs that provide the service along the Rhône Valley to Montpellier and Marseille pass through the Lyon area without stopping. There are six basic services to Montpellier and nine to Marseille. In some cases, separate units for Montpellier and Marseille run as a combined service as far as Avignon where they divide to serve the two destinations. The intermediate towns of Valence, Montelimar and Orange are served by some of these services. A number of services run non-stop between Paris and Avignon in 3 hour 45 minutes (average speed 176 km/h: 109.4 mph) a distance of 658 km (409 miles). One of the Montpellier services runs through to the town of Béziers. Despite the 779 km (484 miles) distance between Paris and Marseille, for which the best journey time is 4 hours 40 minutes, business between these two centres is good and growing.

When the Lyon Contournement is completed in May 1994, all services between Paris and points south of Valence will be accelerated by about 25-30 minutes. Timetables have not yet been finalised, but timings of around 4 hours 10 minutes between Paris and Marseille (non-stop), 4 hours to Montpellier (non-stop to Nîmes), and 3 hours 18 minutes to Avignon are in prospect.

Paris, Toulon and Nice

As SNCF believed most passengers between Paris and the coastal resorts along the Mediterranean Coast would continue to travel overnight, Nice was excluded from the original TGV train service proposals. This decision found little favour with SNCF's customers from the resort towns along the Mediterranean Coast. As most of the traffic is holidaymakers accompanied by considerable volumes of luggage, changing trains at Marseille (St Charles) was particularly unpopular. Following customer complaints and representations from the local authorities along the route, SNCF decided to introduce a through-service between Paris and Nice in April 1987. This now consists of two basic trains per day throughout the year, augmented to four during the summer peak. Journey time of these trains – which have stops at Lyon or Avignon and bypass Marseille altogether – is 7 hours.

Despite the relatively long journey, the two basic Paris–Nice trains load very well even during the winter months. At first, because of pressure on rolling stock resources particularly during the winter sports season, TGV 845 1041 from Paris and TGV 846 1300 from Nice was only formed with a First Class unit. Also, from the start of the 1991-92 timetable, one of these trains has been formed by a single Atlantique set. Unusually, for a long-distance TGV service, both of these trains stop at Lyon Part-Dieu. The purpose of this stop is to create a connection from Lille and other stations in the Nord Region, Rouen and the Ile-de-France, for the Côte d'Azur. TGV 510 from Lille/530 from Rouen arrives at Lyon Part-Dieu at 1151 and TGV 845 leaves for Nice at 1245. There are similar connections northbound. Although the connection is on the long side, it obviates the need to change stations at Paris.

Although TGVs are daytime trains and in principle not suited for long night journeys, two overnight TGVs were in service during the peak of the 1992 summer timetable. TGV 851 departed from Paris at 2302 on Friday nights for Nice returning at 2217 on Sunday and on certain public holiday nights. A more interesting development was an overnight service between Lille and Nice – southbound on Friday and Sunday nights and northbound on Saturday and Monday nights. This was formed by a First Class unit especially equipped with reclinable Second Class seats. The First Class units are of course surplus to business requirements during the peak of the summer season. This service only ran for one season.

Summer-timetable morning service from Paris to Nice passes Arles at the full 200 km/h (125 mph) speed permitted for TGVs on this part of the Rhône Valley route.
Brian Perren

PSE unit 07 heads south through Orange. Parts of the Rhône Valley main line have been upgraded for 200 km/h (125 mph) speed for TGV trains, but the curvature through Orange station necessitates a short restriction of 160 km/h (100 mph).
Michael J Collins

Dijon, Franche-Compté and Lausanne/Bern

TGVs providing this group of services leave the high-speed line at Pasilly from where they use the classic PLM line down into Dijon. Paris to Dijon is the core service with extensions to Besançon in Franche-Compté and the Burgundy towns of Beaune and Chalon-sur-Saône. The international service to Lausanne/ Bern in Switzerland via Vallorbe – provided by the three-voltage units – is part of this group.

With the exception of three services in each direction which only run between Paris and Dijon, most other TGVs on this route are formed with two units for different destinations which divide/combine at Dijon. Journey time from Paris to Dijon is 1 hour 40 minutes. Three trains per day run beyond Dijon along the old PLM main line through Beaune terminating at Chalon-sur-Saône; journey times from Paris are 1 hour 58 minutes and 2 hours 16 minutes. Trains for Dôle, Besançon and Switzerland, take the Jura main line from Dijon. There are four services in each direction between Paris and Besançon; journey time is 2 hours 33 minutes.

There is a basic service of four TGVs between Paris and Lausanne, one of which has a unit for Bern which is detached/attached from/to the train at Frasne. The four trains are branded EuroCity. Journey time from Paris to Lausanne is around 4 hours 45 minutes depending on the number of intermediate stops. For those who may be unfamiliar with the geographical complexities, it should be explained that the border separating France and Switzerland is at Vallorbe and Lausanne is 46 km (29 miles) beyond Vallorbe. As no purpose would be served by terminating SNCF's TGVs – or any other train for that matter – at a small border town such as Vallorbe, the trains run through Switzerland over SBB tracks to Lausanne which is the prime market and where connections can be made for other parts of Switzerland and Italy. Similarly the Paris–Bern TGV crosses the border at Pontarlier – which is 107 km (66 miles) from Bern. There is one TGV from Paris to Bern departing at 1553 (EC429) and 0700 (EC422) from Bern. Journey time between Paris and Bern is around $4^{1}/_{2}$ hours. These services into Switzerland have been very successful.

To emphasise the station's links with a nearby vineyard, a local wine association has erected this sign outside Mâcon-Loché TGV station - Tres Grands Vins Pouilly-Loché and Pouilly Vinzelles. Brian Perren

Alpes Savoie and Geneva

Although the traffic base is more modest, TGV has revolutionised travel between Paris, other parts of France and the Alpes – Savoie, Haute Savoie and the area based on the Geneva conurbation. Access to this area – by road or rail – used to be difficult. During the past few years, new *autoroutes* have been built and improvements made to the rail network including electrification of the single-track branch from Chambéry to the mountain resorts of Albertville and Bourg-St-Maurice. Famed for its mountains and lakes – in particular Mont Blanc, Lake Annecy and Lake Geneva – the area is very popular as an all-season tourist area – skiing and other winter sports from January to April, summer holidays from mid-July to September plus weekenders, many of whom have a second residence in this area. The important centres served by TGV are Geneva, Chambéry (the ancient capital of Savoie), Annecy, Aix-les-Bain and Albertville.

Until 13 December 1992, when the Lyon Contournement opened, TGVs for this area left the LGV just south of Mâcon at the appropriately named Bifurcation Savoie from where they join the old PLM tracks at Pont-de-Veyle. From here the route is through Bourg-en-Bresse, and Ambérieu to Culoz where trains for Geneva turn north to Bellegarde before crossing the border at La Plaine entering Swiss territory to reach Geneva. SNCF operate the route, which is electrified at 1.5 kV dc, right into Geneva station where there are separate 'French' platforms segregated for customs and immigration purposes.

From Culoz trains continue to Aix-les-Bains – the junction for Annecy – and Chambéry. The location of these three towns on the rail network is awkward. To reach Annecy from the Bourg-en-Bresse direction, trains have to reverse in Aix-les-Bains station and there is a voltage changeover at the end of the station platforms as trains move on to the Annecy branch. Only eight miles separate Aix-les-Bains and Chambéry. Because of gradients and curvature between Ambérieu and Chambéry, line speeds are low. Nonetheless, by using the LGV as far as Mâcon, TGV provides very good journey times into the area.

The Paris–Geneva TGV service is a particular success. Before TGV, rail was unable to compete and there are now five services from Paris and six services from Geneva. Journey times vary according to the number of intermediate stops – normally Bellegarde, Bourg-en-Bresse and Mâcon-Loché TGV – and are around 3½ hours. A recent development was the introduction of an early service from Geneva at 0540 arriving in Paris at 0915, aimed at the business traveller. Some trains run non-stop from Bellegarde – connecting station for Annemasse and Evian – to Paris. At peak summer weekends there is a through TGV from Paris to Evian which runs coupled to a Geneva section as far as Bellegarde where it is detached.

With the opening of the Lyon Contournement on 13 December 1992, the service to Chambéry was completely revamped. By remaining on the LGV as far as St-Quentin-Fallavier, using the Lyon–Grenoble line to St-André-le-Gaz and then the branch line thence to Chambéry, it is possible to cut journey times between Paris and Chambéry by about 15 minutes. Not only is the route quicker but – despite the need to reverse direction in Chambéry station – it is now possible to serve Chambéry, Aix-les-Bains and Annecy in that order with one service. Because the distance from Paris to Aix-les-Bains and Annecy via the Lyon Contournement is longer and with the need to reverse at Chambéry, journey times are about the same as the Bourg-en-Bresse route. Unless you have to serve Culoz and Bourg-en-Bresse, the Lyon Contournement routeing is much more efficient.

There are seven services into this area in each direction. Four run via the Lyon Contournement, two of which terminate at Chambéry with the other two going forward (or starting from) Annecy. Three services run between Paris and

Above: **Atlantique sets are used for 'TGV Ski' services to the Alpes during the annual winter sports season.** SNCF

Left: **Many small towns in France enjoy a TGV-service even if this is restricted to two or three trains per day. Beaune - the famous Burgundy wine centre - is a case in point.** Michael J Collins

Annecy, serving intermediate stations including Mâcon-Loché, Bourg-en-Bresse and Aix-les-Bains, where they reverse direction onto the Annecy branch. Journey times from Paris to Chambéry are now around 2 hours 55 mins and 4 hours 50 mins to Annecy.

On basic days there is a total of 12 TGV services to and 13 from the French Alpes area. There are additional services on weekends throughout the year, and during the summer peaks. However, particular mention must be made of the 'TGV Ski'. With some reserve capacity in the TGV fleet during the winter period and with a fast route to the Alpes, SNCF has developed a thriving winter sports market. The key to this success is that the TGVs run direct to the various winter sport stations such as Modane, Bourg-St-Maurice, Albertville, Evian and St-Gervais (for Mont Blanc). Most of these services run to/from Paris but TGVs now run from the Atlantique line (Nantes, Rennes and Poitiers) as well as Lille. Between January and the end of April SNCF moves about 100,000 people on TGV Ski trains.

For a short distance south of Montélimar in Provence, the PLM main line runs alongside the River Rhône. The 'Donzère Gap' is a favoured location for photographers.
Michael J Collins

TGV has considerably improved communications between Paris and other parts of
France including the beautiful Haute Savoie region in the French Alps. There are four
services a day to the all-season resort town at Annecy reached by the single-line
branch from Aix-les-Bains. A two-unit formation is seen near Rumilly. Michael J Collins

8. Atlantique

Atlantique services run from Paris Montparnasse station and serve 31 major and some smaller towns in Brittany and South West France. There are three core routes:

Paris–Rennes, Brest/Quimper
There are 13 basic return services between Paris and Rennes with a best non-stop timing of 2 hours 4 minutes; five of these services run through to the coastal town of Brest, a journey of around 4 hours. To provide a through TGV service from Paris the line from Rennes and Lorient to Quimper has been electrified. The first 180 km (112 miles) was energised in September 1991 when TGVs were extended as far as Lorient, and the second 67 km (42 miles) through from there to Quimper was energised in September 1992. There are five basic services in each direction supplemented at the weekend; journey time is around 4 hours 45 minutes. In some cases two units will work between Paris and Rennes or vice versa, with one unit going through to or starting at Quimper.

Paris–Nantes, Le Croisic
Rail travel between Paris and Nantes – which is the biggest commercial and business centre in Western France – has grown substantially following the launch of TGV in September 1989, when the journey time from Paris was cut to around 2 hours. There are 14 basic return services in each direction; some run through to the resort town of Le Croisic. As is the case at Rennes, some services run with two units as far as Nantes where they divide with one set going forward to Le Croisic. TGVs are permitted to run at 220 km/h over certain sections of the classic route between Le Mans and Nantes.

The important town of Le Mans – which is also the junction station for the Rennes and Nantes lines – has an excellent service to/from Paris. There are 15 basic services in each direction with a journey time of just 55 minutes, *vitesse commerciale* 226.1 km/h (140.5 mph). Given such a dramatic reduction of journey time following the launch of the Atlantique line, Le Mans has generated a commuter traffic of about 350 passengers per day who prefer to live in the local area and work in Paris.

Paris–Tours and Bordeaux
With the introduction of TGV services in September 1990 to the South West-Aquitaine region of France, SNCF's competitive position strengthened considerably. The journey time between Paris and Bordeaux – the focal point of the Aquitaine region – has been reduced by one hour to give a best ever time of 2 hours 54 minutes. With a centre-to-centre journey of around 3 hours, TGV has gained a significant segment of the Paris-Bordeaux business market from its principal competitor Air Inter. There are 15 TGVs in each direction between Paris and Bordeaux, six of which run non-stop in each direction at an average speed of 196 km/h (121.8 mph). A total of seven TGVs run beyond Bordeaux to Tarbes, Toulouse and the Spanish Border at Hendaye. Serving Toulouse via Bordeaux instead of the classic route through Limoges and Brive is an important develop-

This Atlantique service from Paris to Tours is about to stop at Vendôme TGV station. All four tracks through Vendôme - the two platform loops and the two centre tracks - are signalled for full reversible working. The markerboard on the right is for trains travelling in the opposite direction. Brian Perren

ment. Despite the greater distance to Toulouse via Bordeaux, the best 5 hours 5 minutes journey time by TGV is almost one hour quicker; there are three services in each direction which also serve Agen and Montauban.

During the summer peak period, some TGVs are extended from Bordeaux to run to the Atlantic coastal resort town at Arcachon, located at the end of a 19 km branch which diverges from the main line at Facture, 40 km south of Bordeaux.

In addition to the 16 trains between Paris and Bordeaux, there are a further eight services in each direction serving the intermediate towns on the Bordeaux line. Three terminate at Poitiers, four at Tours and one at Angoulême. The Tours trains call at St-Pierre-des-Corps before terminating at Tours station while the Angoulême service terminates there late in the evening to form an early service to Paris on the following morning. Journey time between Paris and Tours (St-Pierre-des-Corps) is 56 minutes; about 300 passengers per day now commute to Paris.

The three Poitiers trains are the nucleus of the intended TGV service through to the important coastal town of La Rochelle when the branch from Poitiers to there is electrified in July 1993; until then connecting diesel-hauled trains of Corail stock provide connections.

The new TGV station built to serve Vendôme – the old town located in the Chateaux de La Loire – is served by four of the Tours trains in each direction. Although only five trains from and four trains to Paris serve this new station – which has been partially funded by the local authority – TGV has transformed the journey time to this town. The 42 minutes timing to Paris is achieved by an average speed of 230.9 km/h (143.7 mph)

No contest! This TGV Atlantique shows its paces as it passes over the competition on the overbridge across the Autoroute Aquitaine. French Railways

Tours station is at the end of a short branch from St-Pierre-des Corps. Some TGVs start from Tours for Paris but at other times an electric push-pull shuttle service, painted in TGV Atlantique livery, provides connections into Bordeaux TGVs at St-Pierre-des-Corps. Brian Perren

To project the TGV image particular care has been given to the design of new stations and refurbishment of older locations. A case in point is this extension to the old station at Nantes. SNCF

With the Atlantique line of route passing close to the town of Vendôme, the local authority collaborated with SNCF to provide a station to serve the area. This attractive building complements the TGV image. SNCF

The 'Petit' Interconnexion

The concept of direct inter-regional TGV services, obviating the need for passengers to change terminal stations in Paris, was introduced in 1985 between Lille and Lyon, and subsequently expanded to include Rouen. During the Ski season, other cross-country TGVs run direct from French provincial centres to the Alpes skiing resorts, but these are restricted to specific weekends.

From 1995, when Le Jonction (Paris Interconnexion) TGV is open, an entirely new network of inter-regional TGVs will be introduced; this will form part of the emerging European high speed network. Meanwhile, with the start of the 1991-92 winter timetable, two services in each direction were introduced between Nantes and Lyon and between Rennes and Lyon. These are referred to as the 'petit interconnexion'. At the same time – and as part of the same service – SNCF commissioned the new outer-suburban TGV railhead station at Massy located to the south west of Paris. .

The three pairs of cross-country trains are formed by Atlantique sets and work as follows.

Rennes / Nantes-Lyon

From the west departures are at 0905 and 1536 from Rennes and 0911 and 1533 from Nantes with return services from Lyon Perrache at 0806 and 1816. With the exception of the morning service from the west which combine at Le Mans, the separate Rennes and Nantes trains couple/uncouple at Massy TGV station. Between Massy TGV (and the Le Mans exception) and Lyon the separate units combine to form a single train through to Lyon.

Tours-Lyon

This service departs from Tours at 0653 (0822 Sundays) and calls at St-Pierre-des-Corps and Massy TGV; return service is at 1635 from Lyon Perrache making the same stops.

After calling at Massy TGV these cross-country TGVs run through the junction onto the Grande Ceinture thence to Valenton where they reverse direction to reach the Sud Est lines at Villeneuve-St-Georges and the PSE line at Lieusaint.

Despite the extra distance involved to the outskirts of Paris, journey time between Nantes and Lyon has been reduced by about two hours to 4 hours 30 minutes; journey time savings from Rennes are even greater. Lyon to Tours is about 1 hour 30 minutes quicker.

Massy TGV: Ile-de-France

The role of Massy – as an outer-suburban railhead for the west of Paris – has already been mentioned, but we should look at the present TGV service in the context of the Ile-de-France region. There are in fact two stations – Massy TGV which is on the TGV line itself and Massy Palaiseau which is on SNCF's Grande Ceinture line – forming this interchange complex. Massy Palaiseau is served by a local SNCF service and also by RER Line B to the centre of Paris, the Gare-du-Nord and Roissy Airport. The Grande Ceinture line is also the route for the TGV from Rouen to Lyon calling at Mantes-la-Jolie, Versailles-Chantiers and Massy Palaiseau. Unfortunately, the position of the two converging routes at Massy is such that the Rouen trains cannot use Massy TGV, calling instead at Massy Palaiseau. Interchange between the SNCF and the RER station is by a footbridge. Facilities at Massy TGV include a bus station, ample car parking, Avis (train + auto) car-hire and a travel centre.

In the latest timetable there are five trains in each direction between Massy and Lyon – three from Massy TGV and two from Massy Palaiseau. There are two

The two power cars from record-breaking trainset No.325 carry commemorative branding. This shot was taken at Bordeaux in September 1990 on the inaugural day of public service.
Brian Perren

The attractive departure hall at Bordeaux St Jean station was refurbished for the launch of TGV Atlantique service.
Brian Perren

each way between Massy TGV and Nantes/Rennes and one each way to/from Tours. There is an early morning service at 0705 from Massy TGV to St-Pierre-des-Corps (for Tours), and stations through to Bordeaux and Irun and two return services from Bordeaux setting down in the late evening.

The Massy station project is an important development, and will do much to encourage the use of rail. Those who live in any of the residential towns to the west of Paris will save at least an hour by using the Massy railhead instead of travelling into the main Paris terminal station.

9. Nord Europe: Le Jonction

Because the distances between Paris and the main centres in Northern France are very much shorter than those to the long-haul destinations in the South East and South West, the characteristics of TGV Nord Europe are quite different. Whereas air is SNCF's main competitor for business travel on the long-haul routes, the car is the main rival so far as Northern France is concerned. Based on previous experience and market research, SNCF is looking for a growth of around 40% following the launch of the Nord Europe domestic TGV service. A total of 5.5 million passengers per year is the aspiration. Most of this business will come from the Lille conurbation plus towns such as Arras, Douai, Valenciennes, Dunkerque and the Calais area. Business is also expected from the nearby Walloon area of Belgium, which is sufficiently close by car or connectional train to Lille to make TGV a viable option for journeys to Paris and beyond.

Given the need to entice potential customers out of their cars – which should not be too difficult with TGV's reputation already established as a prestige travel mode – particular attention has been given for the provision of adequate car parking spaces at railhead stations. There will be 500 spaces at Lille Flandres station and 1,300 at Paris Nord; provision of parking spaces is less of a problem elsewhere. SNCF is also studying the possibility of including a car parking space with the rail ticket; this is one of the items which could be incorporated into the Réserail 2000 system.

Journeys by TGV Nord Europe are very short. Paris Nord to Lille (either the old Flandres or the new Europe station) is exactly 1 hour: an average speed of 227 km/h (141 mph). Other journey times from Paris Nord are 50 minutes to Arras, 1 hour 35 minutes to Valenciennes and 2 hours to Dunkerque. There are 16 (18 at peaks) trains each way between Paris and Lille, some of which will continue to/from Tourcoing, five to/from Valenciennes, five to/from Dunkerque plus one in each direction to/from Arras. Arras has a total of 10 trains per day. TGVs bound for Valenciennes and Dunkerque leave TGV Nord Europe just south of the town where they access the classic tracks to reach the existing station at Arras. Valenciennes trains continue along the classic main line to serve Douai where they diverge to reach the branch to Valenciennes. Most Dunkerque trains will diverge at Arras onto the line through Lens, Béthune and Hazebrouck. The distance from Arras to Dunkerque is 113 km (70 miles). To produce a faster peak journey time, two of the Dunkerque trains will be routed via Lille and Hazebrouck instead of Béthune to give a 1 hour 36 minutes journey time to/from Paris.

Very short journey times will sharpen SNCF's competitive edge to a significant extent, but some problems will have to be resolved. Commuters will undoubtedly be attracted, but whether they will be able to use season tickets on TGV is an issue. The economics of selling discounted tickets on prime heavily-loaded long-distance business trains will undoubtedly have to be resolved through the pricing mechanism. Higher prices for TGV commuters are likely.

To accommodate the TGV Europe, Eurostar and PBKA services, the station layout at Paris-Nord has been substantially modified. Major alterations include extension of platforms to accommodate trains of 400 metres. Regis Chessum

At present the three morning, midday and late afternoon business trains in the Lille (Tourcoing) service are formed of TEE coaches offering a very high standard of classic dining provided by Wagon Lits. The transition to tray meals must be carefully managed. In the mid-1970s SNCF introduced tray meals in the Paris–Lille 'Corail' trains; these proved unpopular to the extent that they were replaced by TEE trains offering the traditional style of service. A very high standard of meal, with a hot main course, has been specified for TGV Nord Europe. In view of the very short time available, staff will have to concentrate on service. There will be no accounting or cash transactions on-board; vouchers for meals, which will include drinks and coffee, will be sold in advance. Bar sales will be in cash, however. Wagons Lits has been awarded the on-board contract for these services.

Control of passengers – for customer-care and revenue protection purposes – is another area of interest. Normally two controllers can deal with 200 passengers in a two-hour journey, but there will be almost 400 people in a Réseau set in a 1 hour journey from Lille to Paris Nord. In theory this would necessitate four controllers, but a system has been devised whereby the First Class passengers will be checked at the doors when they join the train, leaving the team free to check the remainder of the train during the remaining short journey time.

10. Résarail 2000: Reservation and Information Systems

The TGV technology has been matched by equally successful marketing and promotions skills. Everybody in France knows about TGV, even those who may not have used it themselves. The nose and side profile of the trains, together with the TGV logo, is familiar throughout France. Since the launch in 1981, SNCF has successfully cultivated the TGV image as a modern, stylish and user friendly form of travel. Not only is it seen as a prestigious form of transport but it has also generated additional business on SNCF's classic long-distance trains as well as TER regional services. It is a major element in the renaissance of rail travel.

Nonetheless, neither national pride nor speed *per se* is sufficient to sell seats on trains. Today's customers have high and rising expectations which must be recognised and accommodated. TGV is the leader in core markets such as Paris–Lyon, but air is still faster on the longer sectors while door-to-door transport by private car will always score on convenience if not speed.

Recognising that service and customer care must start from the time that the passenger is merely considering the journey, and must be maintained throughout the journey, followed if necessary by after sales attention, SNCF has totally revamped its marketing service to match its TGV product. These innovations are many and varied, and have been developed as experience has been gained with the application of computer technology.

From the start of the 1993 Summer Timetable on 23 May, SNCF's 'Grandes Lignes' business sector changed over to its new Résarail 2000 Reservation and Global Distribution System, although there were considerable difficulties initially in implementing the new technology. The heart of the system is the FFr 138 million 'Socrate' computer centre – reported to be one of the biggest in the world – located at Lille. With all station points-of-sale, the Minitel system and travel agencies on-line, Grande Lignes moved to a Global Distribution System (GDS) enabling it apply yield management techniques to the totality of its business. Henceforth, the price of a TGV ticket is no longer determined by the length of the journey expressed in kilometres, but by a sophisticated system of prices related to the time and date of travel, available capacity, and the market.

Because they are more economic to operate and easier to maintain, most of today's high-speed trains such as the TGV consist of individual rakes of power units and coaches permanently coupled in a fixed-formation. These trains – like aircraft – have a fixed number of seats; no longer can you supply an extra 60 seats on a Friday afternoon simply by attaching an extra coach. With fixed-formation trains, unit capacity varies from 368 seats in a PSE set to 545 seats in the TGV double-deck train now being developed. In other words, do you attach a second unit with 368 seats to a single unit service to cater for 50, 60 or 100 extra passengers, or do you induce them to take an earlier or later train which is undersold and has seats to spare?

A traditional and popular feature of long-distance rail travel is the ability to walk on to a train without the need to book a seat in advance, a facility which coaches and airlines can only offer when a specific seat is available. But today's inter-city trains are not designed to carry standing passengers. To optimise the use of on-board space, most mainland European railways now use open-plan centre-corridor coaches with unidirectional seating. Passengers standing in the centre of a coach are not getting value for money and interfere with the comfort of seated passengers to an unacceptable extent. Access to the bar, train telephone, toilets and the exits is almost impossible in Second Class; catering trolley service is impeded. There is also the issue of safety.

With the launch of the Paris Sud Est TGV in September 1981, in what at the time as seen as a controversial and bold move, compulsory reservation was introduced for all TGV trains. Compulsory reservation – which was introduced through the Résa computerised reservation system introduced in 1973 – was a simple means of distributing demand over timetabled trains. Apart from some supplements and the small reservation fee, differential pricing was not applied at this stage.

With experience gained on the PSE route, SNCF decided to introduce a more sophisticated reservation system for the Atlantique TGV when this was opened in September 1989. Known as Résa 300, it combined the seat reservation with a supplement. Supplements, for prestige services, have been a long-standing feature of SNCF revenue generation, but with Résa 300 the concept was fine tuned to apply as a pricing mechanism to match demand with resources. There are four Résa supplement levels:

Level 1 – for off-peak trains not normally fully loaded
Level 2 – for trains well loaded in First Class but less so in Second Class
Level 3 – for trains well loaded in Second Class but less so in First Class
Level 4 – for peak trains loaded heavily in both First and Second Class

With Résa 300 – which was subsequently extended to the Sud Est TGV and many Grandes Lignes classic routes – each train in the timetable has a separate price, the details of which are published in a colour-coded book for each route including all timetable and facility details.

For the past 15 years airlines have been using Global Distribution Systems with considerable success – in some cases increasing net revenues by about 5% per year. Given the need to compete on an effective basis with internal airlines in France and with the general intention of improving revenue management, in 1987 SNCF began to study the possibility of acquiring a more sophisticated yield management system. An issue was whether its existing Résa system, which was installed in 1973 and which can process 20 transactions per second, was sufficient to handle the growing volume of business as more TGV lines came into service. With the start of the 1993 summer timetable – which featured the opening of the TGV Nord Europe domestic services – 45% of Grande Lignes passengers will be using TGV. If it was necessary to upgrade the 1973 reservation equipment, should the opportunity be taken to acquire new-generation equipment which would enable SNCF to have a complete Global Distribution System.

Yield management techniques are valuable where many types of customer compete for a limited number of seats, where fare values vary, where demand for resources is uncertain or where 'no shows' or cancelled reservations can cause revenue loss. Yield management has enabled airlines to increase revenues by about 5%. Railways, hotels, tour operators and car hire companies are beginning to recognise its value and are now changing to this system. It can only be applied to those services where advanced reservation is necessary and forms part of the basic sales system. It will not work on services which have uncontrolled access through a 'walk on' policy. It is an ideal technique for the TGV system. An appraisal of the potential benefits of moving to yield management through a Global Distribution System, suggested that the rate of return on the admitted high initial outlay was about 15% and would generate additional business to the order of FFr 600 million per year.

Above: **Atlantique units are used for the long journey from Paris to the Mediterranean coast. This shot, taken at Le Trayas is a typical Côte D'Azur scene.**
Voies Ferrees

Typical scene at Paris Gare-de-Lyon. A Sud Est train stands in platform H and an Atlantique in platform I.
Brian Perren

Partnership with American Airlines: Résarail 2000
In March 1989 SNCF decided to replace its original reservation system by adapting American Airlines SABRE and DINAMO software for rail purposes. This decision led to the creation of a joint-venture between SNCF and American Airlines to develop software for rail purposes – Résarail 2000.

Compared with standard rail reservation systems, Résarail 2000 offers a significant step forward. As well as being able to handle up to 800 transactions per second, it can handle much more than basic functions such as reservations and ticketing including:

◆ Complete display of all train categories such as TGV, regional and international trains.

◆ Information on fares and automatic pricing.

◆ 'Bargain Finder' feature which automatically proposes the best fares for passengers.

◆ Availability displays for all types of fare and accommodation categories such as seating or sleeping accommodation, motorail, etc.

◆ Booking capabilities up to 333 days in advance.

◆ Display of commercial information and other services available in stations.

◆ Automatic ticket printing, management of passenger name records, which consists of storing all passenger travel information, class of service, seat, time limit to pick up the ticket etc.

So far as the customer is concerned, the most important change is the combination of the separate train and reservation ticket into a single document at an integrated price. The customer will be offered a fare for each specific service. Broadly speaking prices will remain as now, with higher fares for peak services on busy routes such as Paris–Lyon, and lower prices for less heavily loaded trains. Passengers wishing to pay less will be offered services at less busy times or it will be possible to buy a cheaper ticket which will be offered for a limited period of time after booking for the service opens.

Résarail will considerably simplify information flow. At present a ticket-seller has to consult one or possibly more timetable books before being able to offer the customer a choice of train(s), only to find that the particular train is fully booked when the Résa computer is consulted. With Résarail all features of a journey – train times, availability of seats, price, connecting services, meals etc – can be produced simultaneously on the screen. This facility is made possible by a supplementary computer programme – Multivision – which corresponds to one of the four parts of the seller's VDU display.

From the 1993 summer timetable there are 500 TGVs open for booking for two months so that Résarail will be handling 30,000 trains at any given time. By using the loading history of each of these 30,000 services, each train will be allocated quotas of tickets at different prices according to the level of demand for each train. Thus, the system may refuse to sell a ticket from Montélimar to Marseille on a TGV so as to keep the seat open for a potential Paris to Marseille sale. But even on the busiest trains there will still be a quota of seats which can be discounted, so long as they are booked in advance. The system will also allow some reservations to be made on trains which are theoretically fully booked, but which have a record of 'no shows'; these seats will be discounted.

A long-term possibility is the elimination of the ticket-stamping machines where customers are obliged to 'composte' their tickets before boarding the train. Most passengers find these machines irritating and they do not work too well. They could in future be replaced by intelligent stamping machines, activated by the magnetic line on the ticket, and controlled by the computer. As on the Paris Métro, you would pass the ticket through the slot which would enable you to pass the turnstile giving access to the platform.

SNCF's move to Global Distribution is a watershed in railway ticketing and capacity management, but it is uniquely suited to the French rail market. Only the core route between Paris and Lyon can justify an hourly service throughout the day whereas the service between Paris and Grenoble consists of no more than six trains, none of which have any intermediate stop. On this basis it is perfectly possible to implement a compulsory reservation system without undue customer resistance.

SOCRATE

The massive Socrate computer base – which is located on a site in Lille – is believed to be the largest in the world. There are three main elements in the system:

CRS (Centre des réservation) – This holds a complete listing of all seats available, reservations made and trains carrying compulsory reservations etc. It is operated by two subsidiary computers – Thalès which applies yield management to obtain the best business return and Aristotle for accounting and commercial matters.

SDS (Systeme de Distribution) – SDS is the distribution system advising availability, general information, timetables, fares, travel records, client index and dispatch of documents.

Le Router – This is the communications activity which is the interface with sales terminals (stations, agents, minitel, automatic ticket machines), terminals located abroad, and outside organisations such as train catering contractors, hotels, car hire companies etc.

Estimated cost of the Socrate system is around FFr 1,300 million. Details are FFr 100 million for the site at Lille, FFr 400 for IBM major systems and Teradata database, FFr 400 million for the purchase of 4,500 terminals and around FFr 350-400 million for the purchase of the SABRE software licence from American Airlines. This outlay is equivalent to the cost of 15 TGV trainsets.

Departure indicator board for TGV 8530 1156 from Bordeaux to Paris. The sign says that this service is provided by a single unit. Brian Perren

11. Timetables and Other Facilities

Every effort has been made to ensure that the full range of TGV (and other rail) facilities is widely publicised, easily understood and that all information is readily available for customers. Timetables – the basic railway sales catalogue – have been revamped and reorganised to meet the changing needs brought about by TGV.

SNCF produces national timetable books (the *Indicateur Officiel*) which can be bought by the public – but these are primarily for staff and travel agents. A more suitable timetable book for the regular traveller is the 800 page A5-size *Ville-à-Ville* which sells at FFr 60. Listing all services – direct or by changing – for over 4,000 possible journey opportunities plus a wealth of other basic information, the *Ville-à-Ville* is a model of its kind and sells very well.

However, the most useful booklet for the frequent traveller using a specific route rather than a range of routes, is the A5-size *Guide du Voyageur*. This is now produced for all major trunk routes – TGV and classic services – and is distributed free.

There are several ways of buying a ticket for a TGV (or other rail) journey. Most tickets are sold through SNCF stations, all of which are connected to the SOCRATE computer system or through appointed travel agents who have the same facilities. Having decided your journey needs, the sales clerk consults the Résarail system to check what seats are on offer at what price. The computer will then print and issue the ticket and the whole transaction is completed. Payment by major credit cards is accepted. You can book at any station for any journey. For example, if you are in a small town such as Epernay, you can book seats from Antibes to Paris by TGV without any problem. You can also book and pay for your meal in the First Class at-seat meal-service area if you wish. As all seats on TGV are allocated by computer, seats do not carry reservation tags although every seat is reserved. You locate your seat by reference to your Résa ticket, a seating plan at the end of the coach and the individual seat number.

Two facilities merit special attention. Automatic ticket dispensing machines and 'Minitel'. The automatic dispensers – which are located at selected busy principal stations – work as follows. By pushing the appropriate buttons, you select your destination, day and time of travel, class of travel, seating requirements etc. To complete the transaction you place your credit card into the machine, punch in your PIN and the transaction is completed and the tickets are issued.

Booking by Minitel – which is a French version of the British Prestel system – is basically similar to the automatic dispensers on the stations, except that you make the transaction on your home (or office) terminal. When the transaction is completed you are given a reference number which enables you to collect your tickets at the station prior to departure. You can also make reservation by telephone which you collect and pay for at the station prior to departure.

Seating

Earlier chapters have described the composition and seating configuration on the various TGV types. For passenger information and seat reservation purposes, both PSE and Atlantique sets are numbered from 1 upwards starting with the first vehicle from the platform buffer stops end at Paris. Trains starting from the provinces are numbered in reverse order. Coach reservation numbers are the same as the formation numbers – that is R1 to R8 in PSE sets are coaches 1 to 8 for public purposes and R1 to R10 in Atlantique sets are coaches 1 to 10. When a train consists of two units the rear unit leaving Paris remains the same and the leading unit vehicles are numbered from 11 to 18 in the case of PSE sets or 11 to 20 for Atlantique sets; reverse order applies for trains starting from the provinces bound for Paris. Like BR's InterCity trains the First Class is always at the buffer-stop end leaving Paris, but not if there are two units.

PSE, Atlantique, Réseau and 2N sets all have a space for a disabled passenger and their wheelchair in coach R1. This is reserved in the same way as other seats.

Catering for the needs of families is an important item. There are two products aimed at this market – special facilities for families travelling together and a separate scheme for conveying unaccompanied minors.

There are two family areas on TGV Atlantique – *Espace Familles* and *Espace Enfants*. Espace Familles consists of four bays of conventional Second Class face-to-face seating, but with a small fifth tip-up seat fixed to the side of the coach to form a carré (or square) of five seats. The two toilets in the same area have been modified to include facilities such as nappy changing. Two bays of seats are in coach 8, two are in the adjoining end of coach 9 with the toilet located in the space over the articulated bogie supporting the ends of coach 8 and 9. Seating in *Espace Familles* is sold through the normal TGV reservation system, but if by a certain date no families have booked, the seats are sold for Standard Class passengers.

Espace Enfants is a small social area designed for older children and is located at the outer end of coach 10 adjoining the power car. Because the Atlantique sets have only four motor bogies as opposed to six in the Paris Sud Est (and Eurostar) sets, the space at the outer ends of the rake – which would have otherwise been necessary to house the motor block for the two outer end motor bogies – is available for other use. At the Second Class end of the train the space is used for Espace Enfants; no charge is made for this facility.

Family facilities are also provided in the new build of Réseau sets. There are no family facilities in the original PSE sets; this is an important gap in the family offer which SNCF will doubtless address when these trains become due for their mid-life major refurbishment.

For many years international airlines have conveyed unaccompanied minors – referred to in the trade as UMs – as part of the basic offer without extra charge. As airline passengers are closely supervised from the point of check-in through to the end of the flight, this does not pose any particular problems. Recognising the need for a similar type of service, SNCF offers a young travellers service marketed under the brand name of *Jeune Voyageur Service* (JVS). It works as follows. On specific dates advertised in the public timetable, groups of up to 10 children are escorted by a qualified person, and delivered to a nominated person at the arrival station. JVS is only available by advance booking. Customers using the service must show legal proof of identity and relationship with the child and similar documentation has to be produced when the child is handed over to the recipient at the end of the journey. Children must be presented to the courier at least 30 minutes before departure time and each child must carry its own luggage which is restricted to a maximum of seven kilos. The courier is responsible for the safety and entertainment of the child throughout the journey.

12. 'Le Bon Moment': TGV Catering

As the Sud Est project began to take shape, it became apparent to SNCF that a major revamp of train catering and on-board service would be necessary to meet the totally changed conditions of travel created by TGV. With greatly reduced journey times, vastly increased numbers of passengers, higher-density seating, less space for food preparation and storage plus the intensive use of trainsets, an airline-type modular system was the only practical option.

This change of philosophy – and the need for a complete break with past practice – is best explained by reference to the old TEE 'Mistral' service between Paris, Lyon, Marseille and Nice. Provided by Wagon Lits, the train offered excellent food and service in an atmosphere of elegance and style. At its peak the 'Mistral' had a catering staff of around 16; all food for the four-course lunch and five-course dinner was prepared and cooked on the train. Meal prices compared favourably with terra-firma restaurants of similar quality, but while the cost of providing a lavish service on this scale was very high it was necessary to protect First Class ticket sales. By the late 1970s, the old TEEs – excellent though they were – had lost a lot of custom to the airlines and its market had started a long-term decline. Clearly this style of high-profile service was not appropriate for TGV.

Lunch service in Atlantique 'Club Duo' by Serviar.

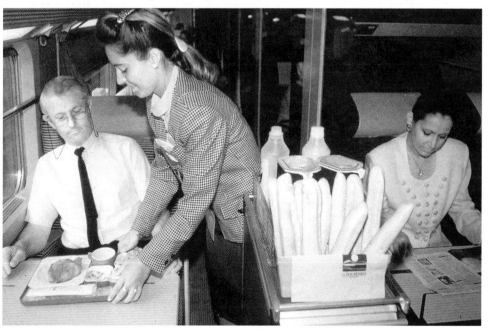

In France, on-board food and drink service is not provided by SNCF, but is awarded to outside caterers under long-term contracts obtained by competitive tender. There are three companies – Wagon Lits, Servair and a small enterprise AuverRail who operate on classic trains out of Clermont Ferrand. Wagon Lits – who have been in rail catering since 1882 – have 65% of SNCF's business including the entire PSE and Nord Europe domestic network. Servair – the catering affiliate of Air France – have 32% of the total including the Atlantique TGV network. As the catering turnover is less than the cost of providing the service, SNCF supports catering in order to protect passenger revenue. It is an essential feature of the total rail product. Thus, these catering services – all of which have a common branding 'Le Bon Moment' – are closely monitored by SNCF. Evidence that a high standard of service is being provided was confirmed by recent market research which showed that 82% of passengers were satisfied with the full meal service, 80% with the bar and 73% with the train trolley service.

The contract to provide the food and drink service on the Paris Sud Est TGV was awarded to Wagon Lits, at that time the only realistic contender; the Atlantique-line contract was awarded to Servair. Because of the scale of the investment to launch the large and complex Sud Est catering operation – which involved construction of a new FFr 50 million depot near the Gare-de-Lyon terminus – the contract is long-term.

Partly to create a new image and also to separate the TGV operation from its other rail services, Wagon Lits created a separate subsidiary company known as Sorenolif. Originally, Sorenolif used the brand name Service 260; this is now replaced by 'Le Bon Moment' Wagon Lits.

Food service on TGV comprises full meals at-seat in First Class and a bar for snacks and drinks for other customers; on some services a cold-meal tray service is also offered in Second Class. This service is provided by a system based on a successful marriage of rail and aircraft catering practices. All supplies are loaded into modules in the supply depot and taken alongside the train by tractors where they are loaded on board. Modules for First Class are loaded through a door adjoining the small galley over the bogie between coaches R1 and R2 and the bar supplies through a similar door in coach R4. Full meals are served only at appropriate times, but bars are always open. When two TGVs run coupled both bars will be in use, but meal service may not necessarily be duplicated. To ensure meal service, passengers can reserve in advance.

In accordance with French gastronomic traditions, particular attention is given to the quality of the food and drink. Despite the limitations imposed by tray service, standards are very high. On the Sud Est, Wagon Lits serve a four-course meal for lunch or dinner consisting of an entrée; fish, meat or poultry main course with vegetable or alternatively a grilled meat main course; a cheese course and dessert. Typically this could consist of: melon and parma ham, trout and potatoes or rump steak, camembert and pastry. A cold meal is also offered. Menus – which are the same for lunch and dinner – are changed every day with up to 50 combinations in normal rotation. However, if you take lunch and dinner on the same day the menu is the same, but you do have the choice of the alternative main course or the completely separate cold meal tray. Hot courses are pre-cooked and reheated on the train without significant diminution of quality.

For its Paris Sud Est operation, Wagon Lits employs a staff of around 1,000 people who provide an annual service of 64,801 bar journeys and 23,895 main meal journeys. In 1990, a total of 152,900 breakfasts and 356,000 lunch/dinners were served. Bar sales comprised 1.3 million sandwiches or pastries, 0.5 million hot snacks and 6.7 million hot or cold drinks. Total turnover on the entire operation was FFr 266 million.

Sud Est at-seat meal service by Wagon Lits.

Maintaining standards in restricted surroundings requires a high level of staff training and motivation. Also, mindful that many of its customers – particularly between Paris and Lyon – travel once or twice each and every week, it is essential that the food is varied and the service itself is always fresh. So, with the objective of refreshing not only the content of its menus but also its style and overall ambience, Wagon Lits decided to introduce a major revision of PSE service as its contribution to the TGV 10th Anniversary Celebrations in October 1991.

All aspects of service were revamped. Staff went on updated training refresher courses and were issued with new style uniforms. These are part of a co-ordinated visual design which has also been applied to the meal tray and certain items such as a new larger oval-shape plate for the main course. Food content has been revised with a new range of dishes, and a wider choice of cheeses and desserts. This new service applies to all PSE routes, with the exception of the EC23 'Cisalpin' 1221 Paris to Lausanne. In response to requests from its Swiss clientele, Wagon Lits introduced a new Pullman-style service on this train with new menus. So that these meals could be served with greater comfort for the passenger, clip-on extensions were added to the standard TGV fold-down tables. Some of the ideas used in the 'Cisalpin' service were carried into the new 10th Anniversary format.

Servair entered the rail catering business in 1973 when they were awarded the contract for the Cherbourg and Le Havre routes; in 1980 they took over services from Paris Montparnasse to Western France followed by service from Paris Austerlitz in 1985. In 1987 they won the tender for the Atlantique TGV network.

The Atlantique catering operation – which is identical in concept to the PSE – operates from a new purpose-built rail catering centre at the Vaugiraud section of Paris Montparnasse terminal station. Costing FFr 100 million, the three storey depot has 9000 sq metres of space; there is a staff of 530 of whom 260 work on-board the trains. Annual sales consist of 350,000 breakfasts, 650,000 lunch/dinners and eight million bar sales; turnover is around FFr 270 million.

Like the PSE, all Atlantique TGVs have bar service throughout the journey plus at-seat full meal service in First Class. TGVs serving full meals – which can be booked in advance – are shown in the timetable publications.

13. The Sud Est Postal Trains

An interesting feature is the service provided by purpose-built TGV postal trains to carry mail for La Poste (French Post Office) between Paris and Lyon. As the PSE project began to take shape, La Poste expressed interest in the possibility of using TGV for the carriage of light postal traffic and so continuing the long-standing arrangements with SNCF for the carriage of mail in specially adapted stock.

Agreement was reached whereby La Poste would finance the construction of $2^1/_2$ TGV sets, the details of which are given in an earlier chapter. The postal TGV started on 1 October 1984, and replaced an overnight air service between Paris and Lyon, previously provided by two Transoll 160 aircraft. The payload of a postal TGV is 88 tonnes compared with 14.3 tonnes on the Transoll 160.

Technically the postal sets are identical to the passenger trains, but there are no windows, passenger doors or seats. Internally the space has been used for the storage of trolleys conveying sacks of mail; access is through a door in the side of each vehicle. The sets are painted in the standard French Post Office yellow and grey livery. To provide cover for maintenance, postal trains are built as half-sets, a power car plus four articulated coaches which are numbered from one to five. Sometimes Post Office power cars have been used to substitute for standard power cars in passenger sets.

There are two daytime and two night services in each direction. Departures are at 1941 and 2230 from Paris-Charolais postal depot and at 0944 and 2325 from Lyon Montrochet postal station. The two night services both call at Mâcon-Vinzelles postal station to exchange mail with other Sud Est trains. The postal TGVs are part of a complex distribution network covering the whole of South East France involving air, road and other SNCF services. Mâcon-Vinzelles postal station is located on the single-line connection between the LGV and PLM lines at Mâcon. The overnight north and southbound postal TGVs use the PLM line between Créches-sur-Saône and Lyon Montrochet to avoid a reversal en route.

Upper right: **Sud Est postal TGV.** Paul Billet

Right: **La Poste logo.** SNCF

LA POSTE

TGV P R41 30

14. TGV Operations

The commercial success of TGV owes much to the production side of SNCF (Direction du Transport) who converted the aspirations of the business side of the organisation (Direction Grandes Lignes) into robust and viable operating plans. This work is based on three objectives: design of a train service which meets customer expectations with regard to journey times, frequency and pricing; creation of the conditions for the implementation of operating systems and monitoring day-to-day performance; and meeting of very strict safety criteria.

Development of the TGV network goes far beyond the relatively straight-forward task of building a new line and ordering a fleet of high-speed trains. As emphasised in earlier chapters, the TGV system is not a self-contained operation, but has been designed so that trains can use the high-speed line to access the entire network, provided the routes are electrified. So, in addition to the investment in high-speed lines and trainsets, a parallel programme of major works was implemented to prepare key points in the classic network to handle the new services having particular regard to higher levels of traffic density which TGV would generate.

For the 1981 Paris Sud Est project, associated works included major changes to the Gare-de-Lyon station in Paris, remodelling of the approach tracks and reducing the signalling headways out to the start of the new line at Lieusaint. A new station was built at Lyon Part-Dieu together with associated track work necessitating the construction of several grade-separated junctions. Many other lines were upgraded with strengthened tracks and catenary, improved traction current supplies and resignalled for higher speeds. Platform lengths at many stations were extended to handle two-unit 400-metre TGV services. The lines from Lyon to Grenoble and from Chambéry to Bourg-Saint-Maurice have been electrified so that TGVs can be accepted.

A similar programme of associated works for the Atlantique TGV was also undertaken. Highlights were the rebuilding of Paris Montparnasse terminal station; modification of the track, catenary and signalling so that TGVs can travel at speeds up to 220 km/h on some existing classic lines; and extension of electrification so that TGVs can run through to Brest, Quimper, Le Croisic and La Rochelle.

In preparation for TGV Nord Europe services to Lille and the Nord-Pas-de-Calais region, Eurostar to London and the Brussels-Cologne-Amsterdam service, there are major works at Paris Nord terminal station. These include the re-modelling of the station layout, platform extensions and passenger handling facilities. Work at other locations in Northern France is also in progress.

Before describing TGV operations in greater detail, some general points about the structure of SNCF 'Grandes Lignes' services would be helpful. Because the population of France is thinly spread over a large geographical area, there are very few major centres of population – the greater Paris area, the Lyon conurbation, the Lille conurbation and the area around Marseille. There are many important smaller centres in France – Bordeaux, Nantes, Rennes, Grenoble and Strasbourg – but these are small compared with provincial centres in Britain and Germany. Moreover, the distance between the major centres is quite considerable. Paris to Lyon is about 275 miles and Lyon to Marseille is about 250 miles. Lille to Lyon is about 450 miles. In contrast, Paris to Lille is only 120 miles. Another important factor is that most traffic flows in France (road as well as rail) tend to radiate from Paris, although cross-country connections are being improved. The cross-country TGV network – *La Jonction* – will make an important contribution in this regard.

Railways exist to move people (or freight) and the first consideration must always be the market. Given a population spread which is relatively thin, passenger traffic flows in France vary to a considerable extent. Thus, with the exception of Paris–Lyon, long-distance services in France are not organised on a regular-interval basis with an hourly (or half-hourly) frequency across the country as is the case in more densely-populated countries such as Britain, Belgium, the Netherlands, Germany and Switzerland. Instead most points on the TGV network have five or six trains a day to/from Paris. To cover these markets in the most cost-effective way, services are designed to take the maximum number of passengers to groups of stations in block loads. Concentrating traffic flows in this way enables trains to run from Paris for considerable distances before making their first intermediate stop to set down passengers.

Another general point regarding SNCF operating policy is the question of covering peak demand. Because land is comparatively cheap in France, many French families of fairly modest means own a second home in the provinces and many French people have strong roots in the country. These are the reasons for the widespread popularity of 'le weekend'. While SNCF charges higher fares for peak times such as Friday afternoon and Sunday evening, a significant reserve capacity – particularly trainsets – is still retained to meet these peak periods.

While these basic tenets remain, TGV has totally transformed the travel market between the greater Paris area and the Lyon conurbation. These two major centres are 275 miles apart – roughly the same distance as London to Newcastle – but now the journey time is just 2 hours it is the time factor rather than the distance factor which is motivating the market. Traffic between Paris and Lyon has grown to the extent that there is now a total of 23 TGVs in each direction on basic days, increased to 27 on Fridays. Given this level of frequency, a regular-interval service is the best way to organise the timetable. With the exception of the 'white period' discussed later, the service to Lyon is hourly at fixed times throughout most of the day, with more frequent departures in the peak periods.

In contrast to Paris–Lyon, the frequency to other parts of South East France is comparatively low. There are 10 trains each way to Dijon, of which two run through to Chalon-sur-Saône, four to Besançon and four to Lausanne/Bern. There are five each way to Geneva, five to the Savoy Alpes (Chambéry and Annecy), five to Grenoble and 13 to points south of Lyon along the Rhône Valley to Avignon, Montpellier, Marseille, Toulon and Nice. Together with four cross-country services from Tours, Nantes/Rennes and Lille/Rouen to Lyon which join the Sud Est network at Villeneuve-St-Georges, there is a total of 66 trains per day in each direction over the Sud Est Ligne à Grande Vitesse as far as Pasilly junction where the branch to Aisy for Dijon leaves the main line to Sathonay (Lyon) or St-Quentin-Fallavier.

From the Gare-de-Lyon terminal station in Paris through to the exit points from the Ligne à Grande Vitesse – Aisy (for Dijon, Franche Compté and Lausanne/Bern), Pont-de-Veyle (for Geneva), Sathonay (for Lyon, the Rhône Valley and the Mediterranean Coast), St-Quentin-Fallavier (for Grenoble and the Savoy Alpes) – the entire Sud Est TGV service is timetabled over one track in each direction. For the first 29 km (18 miles) from the Gare-de-Lyon to the start of the LGV at Lieusaint and from the four aforementioned interface points where TGVs rejoin the classic network, TGVs share tracks with other express and regional passenger services and with freight trains.

Although Sud Est, Atlantique and Réseau trainsets use the Sud Est line, for the present all trains will run at a maximum speed of 270 km/h between

Lieusaint and Sathonay. However, 300 km/h is possible over the Sud Est extension from Montanay to St-Quentin-Fallavier enabling Atlantique or Réseau sets to run at their full speed potential. At present operating headway is five minutes between consecutive trains at 270 km/h.

Point-to-point running times for the Sud Est line produce basic journey times of 2 hours between Paris (Gare-de-Lyon) and Lyon (Part-Dieu) - see opposite. These basic running times produce journeys of 1 hour 37 minutes to Dijon, 1 hour 39 minutes to Mâcon-Loché and 2 hours 54 minutes to Grenoble. The full schedule between Paris and Grenoble is shown in the tables. To allow for the tortuous exit from the Gare-de-Lyon platforms and for speed restrictions between Villeneuve-St-Georges and Brunoy, 15 minutes is allowed for the initial 29.4 km to Lieusaint; similarly seven minutes is the schedule for the 8.5 km from the end of the LGV at Sathonay through to Lyon Part-Dieu station. Thus, the pass-to-pass time over the 389.3 km from Lieusaint to Sathonay is 98 minutes, an average speed of 246.8 km/h (153.4 mph). This schedule has a margin of six minutes to offset the effects of unforeseen delays.

As described in chapter 4, the present theoretical capacity of the PSE line is 12 trains per hour for 15 hours per day, giving a daily total of 180 trains in each direction. While this level of throughput between Lieusaint and Sathonay/St-Quentin-Fallavier is perfectly possible, the actual number of TGVs which can be operated is more likely to be constrained by the capacity at key points on the classic network. There is also the issue of the 'white period'.

Because SNCF's engineers feel that certain essential engineering inspections can only be undertaken in daylight, most main lines in France have a period of about 1½ hours when the line is closed and no trains are run. This shutdown is known as the 'white period', so called because of the blank space on the timetable graph. To meet the needs of the 'white period' there are no TGV departures from the Gare-de-Lyon between 0815 and 1000 or between 1200 and 1330 from Lyon Part-Dieu.

This Lyon to Paris train leans to the curve as it passes through Mâcon-Loché TGV station at the full 270 km/h line speed. Note the Markerboards.
Brian Perren

PARIS SUD EST STANDARD SCHEDULE: PARIS (GARE DE LYON) - LYON (PART-DIEU)

	Km Points	Cumulative point-to-point times (mins)	Cumulative km
Paris (Gare-de-Lyon)	-	0	-
La Vert Maison	8.1	6	8.1
Villeneuve-St-Georges	14.3	8	14.3
Brunoy	21.1	11	21.1
Lieusaint Junction	29.4	15	29.4
PRS10 Moissy	2.1	15	31.5
PRS11 Le Châtelet	25.9	21	55.3
PRS12 Marolles	49.2	27	78.6
PRS13 Cuy	71.4	32	100.8
PRS14 Vaumort	92.7	38	122.1
PRS15 Verigny	117.0	44	146.4
PRS16 Tonnerre	139.8	50	169.2
PRS17 Pasilly Junction	162.1	55	191.5
PRS18 Toutry	182.0	60	211.4
PRS19 Lacour D'Arcenay	202.3	65	231.7
PRS20 Vianges	225.8	71	255.2
PRS21 Sully	247.4	76	276.8
PRS22 Montchanin	273.7	82	303.1
PRS23 Vaux-En-Pré	292.9	87	322.3
PRS24 Cluny	315.5	92	344.9
PRS25 Mâcon-Loché	333.9	97	363.3
Bifurcation Savoie	337.7	98	367.1
PRS27 Cesseins	341.1	104	370.5
Montanay Bifurcation	380.5	109	409.9
PK 386	386.0	111	415.4
Sathonay station	389.3	113	418.7
St Clair Junction		117	-
Lyon Part-Dieu: flyover	505.2	118	-
station	507.5	120	427.2

Paris (Gare-de-Lyon) - Lyon (Par-Dieu) 120 mins
Average speed: 213.6 km/h (132.7 mph)

PARIS SUD EST STANDARD SCHEDULE: PARIS (GARE DE LYON)-GRENOBLE (1)

	Km points	Cumulative time (mins.)	Cumulative kms
Montanay Junction	380.5	109 (2)	409.9
PRS 41 Miribel	389.1	111	418.5
Satolas station	409.7	117	439.1
Grenay Junction (3)	418.5	120	447.9
St-Quentin-Fallavier (4)	419.9	120	449.3
Bourgoin-Jallieu	41.6	128	464.8
La Tour Du Pin	56.6	135	479.8
Saint André Le Gaz	63.4	138	486.6
Chabons	79.4	147	502.6
Voiron	105.2	160	528.4
Le Chartreux	117.9	167	541.1
Saint Egreve	124.2	170	547.4
Grenoble station	130.5	175	553.7

Paris (Gare-de-Lyon)-Grenoble 175 minutes. Average speed 189.8 km/h (118 mph)

(1) See above for timings from Paris to Montanay
(2) Passing time
(3) Grenay, 418.5 km from the start of the LGV at Lieusaint, is the point where the spur to the Grenoble line leaves   the Lyon Contournement which will continue to Valence from 1994.
(4) St-Quentin-Fallavier is the point where the spur from the LGV joins the Lyon to Grenoble line at km point 24.7

Another feature influencing line capacity is the effect of trains calling at the two intermediate stations at Le Creusot and Mâcon-Loché. The time taken to decelerate from 270 km/h to a stand in the station platforms, two minutes dwell time, plus the time to regain the 270 km/h line speed from a standing start, costs a total of about eight minutes. Thus, trains stopping at either of these stations occupy the equivalent of two train paths.

The Gare-de-Lyon terminal station in Paris is a key location. With the exception of the five cross-country services which come on to the network at Villeneuve-St-Georges, all PSE services use the Gare-de-Lyon. Between 1980 and 1982 the layout at the station was substantially modified. A new four-platform sub-surface station for suburban trains was built enabling space to be released on the 'arrival' side of the main station. Hitherto, the old Gare-de-Lyon layout was divided into separate arrival and departure platforms; only a few platforms could be used for 'in-and-out' working. All main line trains were taken to the sidings for servicing before moving back to the terminal for their return journeys. Today there is a total of 24 platforms – four sub-surface sharing a spacious circulating area with RER A, 12 platforms lettered A to M on the old arrival side and eight platforms, 12 to 19, on the old departure side.

The major change involved platforms A to M. These can now be used for either arrivals or departures. There is an inspection pit in each track so that the underside of trains can be checked between journeys. A number of TGVs use these platforms for 'in-and-out-working' returning to traffic shortly after a brief layover for maintenance and cleaning. Platforms 12 to 19 are still regarded as departure tracks; trains from the servicing sidings at Bercy reach these platforms over a flyover to avoid confliction. It is possible for an incoming TGV to run into platforms 12 to 19, but this is a slow and complicated manoeuvre which loses time and blocks departures from other platforms.

The busiest days of the year at the Gare-de-Lyon are on Fridays throughout most of the year, on days preceding public holidays and on Saturdays between Christmas and the end of April during the annual trek to the Alpes for ski holidays. For normal business travel the busiest period is Monday to Friday between 0615 and 0815 when 12 important business trains are despatched; five of these are formed with two and the remainder with single units, a total of 17 units offering 6,300 seats. Thus, another aspect of TGV capacity is the ability of the station facilities – Métro, RER, taxis, buses, cars, buffets, shops and ticket selling points – to handle the passage of these people. From 0800 the activity of the station switches to the arrival side when a group of nine TGVs from the provinces are scheduled to arrive by 0930.

Platform occupation is the critical factor at the Gare-de-Lyon. On the face of things, 20 platforms – which are also used by longer-distance commuter trains and locomotive-hauled services to points on the old (PLM) line to Dijon and to Clermont Ferrand – would seem to be sufficient for the level of service. About 25 minutes is required to empty and check out an incoming train before it can go empty to Bercy Conflans sidings. Allowing a margin for late running, this means that each platform can cope with two arrivals per hour; two departures an hour are also possible. On this basis it would not be possible to handle 12 TGVs per hour – plus other services – for other than short bursts of activity. Another issue is the ability of the reception sidings at Bercy to receive and process trains through the depot. Careful planning of the Gare-de-Lyon station working is therefore an essential part of the Sud Est TGV train plan.

Train working at Lyon also requires careful planning. Because the alignment brought the new railway into the area at Sathonay and not by the old route into Lyon Perrache, a new station had to be built at Part-Dieu. This was located at a point where a wide range of connections between TGV from Paris (and elsewhere) could be made with local, regional and cross-country services which feed into Lyon. Lyon is the hub of the SNCF national network. The old station at Lyon Perrache – the layout of which is constrained by short platforms and a long tunnel at the north end – was unsuitable for the level of traffic generated by TGV.

While an extensive programme of new works including strategically placed grade-separated junctions was initiated to segregate traffic flows and eliminate potential conflictions, traffic density in the Lyon area is an on-going problem. However, the opening of the Rhône Alpes TGV (the Lyon Contournement) will provide relief. From 13 December 1992, all Paris–Grenoble plus some Chambéry TGVs were transferred to the northern section of the new line through to St-Quentin-Fallavier where they now access the Grenoble line. Coupling/uncoupling Grenoble portions from the Lyon Perrache units at Part-Dieu station is now discontinued. This first stage has removed five TGVs in each direction from the Lyon area, but the major benefit will come in 1994 when the Contournement opens up to Valence. All TGVs from Paris along the Rhône Valley to Avignon, Montpellier, Marseille and Nice – a total of 13 trains in each direction – will be diverted away from the congested Lyon area.

Another major challenge for SNCF's timetable specialists was scheduling paths for TGVs over the 144 miles of route between Lyon and Avignon. There are two pairs of tracks – one on either side of the River Rhône – between Lyon and Avignon. On average some 124 trains (including 30 or so TGVs) are scheduled to run on the right (i.e. east) bank of the Rhône between 0600 and 2200. This flow is a mix of regional passenger trains stopping every 15 to 20 km (9 to 12 miles) with a mean speed of about 75 km/h (46 mph), freight trains with maximum speeds of 100/120 km/h (62/74 mph), some 160 km/h (100 mph) locomotive-hauled express services, to which 13 or so TGVs in each direction running over some sections of track at 200 km/h (125 mph) have to be superimposed. As was the case at Lyon, a major study of traffic flows and timetabling options had to be undertaken as an essential preliminary to the recast of the entire train working plan in this area.

To minimise the impact on line capacity, TGVs running along the Rhône Valley corridor have mostly been 'flighted' whereby paths are plotted for two or even three consecutive trains to/from separate destinations. Three departures from Paris – 1010 to Montpellier (TGV 861), 1023 to Marseille (TGV 811) and 1041 to Nice (TGV 845) – all pass along the route at very close intervals. By the time they approach Avignon, there is only a few minutes between these three trains. Similarly, in the reverse direction on peak days, two trains – 1358 (TGV 824) from Marseille and 1404 (TGV 874) from Montpellier – run non-stop from Avignon to Paris at a headway of seven minutes. A distance of 658 km (408 miles), makes it the longest non-stop rail journey in Europe and probably the world!

Outside Paris, Lyon and the Rhône Valley are the busiest parts of the SNCF network, but even the lower-density routes served by TGVs pose problems. EuroCity TGVs between Paris and Lausanne/Bern use single-track sections of route between Dôle and Vallorbe. Another section of single-line track is the 44 km (27 miles) between St-André-le-Gaz and Chambéry. With the opening of the Lyon Contournement, the four TGVs in each direction between Paris and Chambéry which have been diverted away from the Bourg-en-Bresse route will use this branch, but traffic density is low and no particular problems are foreseen. The other route into the Alpes which leaves the LGV near Mâcon (Bifurcation Savoie) is also a problem. Line speeds between Ambérieu and Culoz are restricted by gradients and track geometry and the line has to be shared with a significant flow of international freight traffic up to the Italian border station at Modane. With the opening of the Lyon Contournement the number of TGVs using this line has been reduced; apart from two services to Annecy only Geneva TGVs remain.

As they gained experience during the early years of operation, SNCF's rolling stock engineers progressively raised the productivity of the Sud Est TGV fleet. Higher levels of safety, reliability and availability have exceeded targets set when the first trains in the new fleet were commissioned and entered revenue-earning service. Given intensive use at very much higher speeds than ever before, monitoring and inspection rules had to be completely revised. To cope with TGV design features – articulated trainsets, pressure-tight toilets etc – purpose-built maintenance facilities had to be provided. These were designed to reconcile the objectives of safe operation, high availability and low rates of in-service failure and down time for maintenance.

Maintenance of the fleet is based on a 'contract' between the mechanical engineering and operating departments. This specifies the number of trainsets to be available for service for each timetable period, days of each week etc. Timetables and workshop capacity are co-ordinated. Maintenance of Sud Est trainsets is divided between the main works at Bischheim (near Strasbourg) and the maintenance facility at Villeneuve-St-Georges, known as *Atelier Materiel Paris Sud Est* (AMPSE). Bischheim is responsible for the overhaul of all major components as well as bodyshell frames. Trains visit Bischheim works for major overhaul and refurbishment which normally takes about four weeks.

Working on two eight-hour shifts, AMPSE carries out work which requires stopping a trainset for a full day or longer, periodic inspections, component changes, repairs and modifications. Facilities include inspection pits, wheel lathes, a drop table and a simultaneous lifting facility whereby the entire eight-car rake can be lifted off its bogies. With modular components maintenance down time is minimised.

Lower-level maintenance is carried out in the Gare-de-Lyon terminal station or at the nearby servicing depot at Bercy Conflans. Work in the Gare-de-Lyon is smaller scale and is carried out between journeys. Bercy Conflans is open on the 24-hour basis for scheduled but less important maintenance, repairs, cleaning and trainset preparation. Trains are of course stabled overnight at points in the provinces but only routine cleaning is carried out before they return to Paris.

Having determined the number of trainsets that can be made available for service at particular times, the next task is to weave the work of these units into the fabric of the timetable plan. Reconciling the desire to maximise the use of these specialist high-tech trains against the discipline imposed by the needs of the maintenance cycle is a difficult task. The nature of the PSE service is such that all trains either depart from or return to Paris at least once per day; some trains make two return trips into and out of Paris. Rosters must allow for the maintenance cycle (see panel opposite top) to be met at the specified time or accumulation of kilometres.

Deployment of individual trainsets is by means of a system of work 'days' through which trainsets cycle; the cycle provides time for visits to Bercy Conflans for various levels of short-term maintenance. The cycles do not allow for extended visits for major maintenance.

As well as meeting the constraints of the maintenance cycle, there is also the issue of trainset positioning. Matching arrivals with return services is not a problem on high-density routes such as Paris to Lyon, but as demand for TGV services to more remote or distant parts of the national network has increased positioning had become more critical. Paris to Nice is a good case in point.

Outside the summer peak there are two daily services in each direction, the times of which are chosen to suit the needs of a prime target market: the leisure traveller.

Departures from Paris are at 1041 and 1320 arriving in Nice at 1738 and 2022; departures from Nice are at 1008 and 1300 arriving in Paris at 1709 and 1951. As

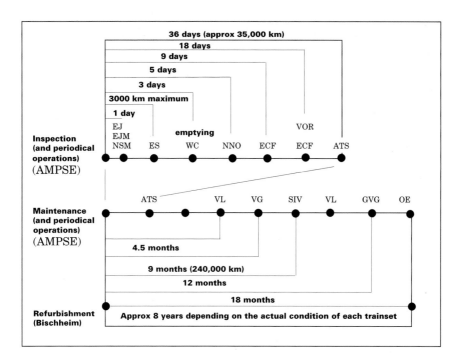

there is no further scope to use these trains both have to stand overnight at Nice for over 16 hours. In complete contrast there is one roster which calls for two return trips from Paris to Lyon, a total of 1728 km (1074 miles) within a span of 12 hours.

The Lyon Contournement timetable – from 13 December 1992 to 22 May 1993 – shows how day-to-day fluctuations in demand affect trainset utilisation. As well as running additional services, the timetable period also covers the 'TGV Ski' services which applied on Saturdays and Sundays from December to the end of April. To cope with traffic growth both prior to and after the opening of the Contournement, a number of Atlantique trainsets have been allocated to support the Sud Est fleet. These are serviced and cleaned at Bercy Conflans, but returned to their base at Châtillon every few days for more detailed maintenance. The trainsets are not dedicated to the Sud Est and are part of the basic Atlantique fleet. While this back-up is very welcome, only Lyon Part-Dieu, Lyon Perrache and Grenoble can accommodate two Atlantique trainsets coupled for multiple-unit working.

A total of 76 sets is needed to cover the basic Tuesday to Thursday service, the pattern of which is largely determined by business travel. A Further 25 sets are pressed into service on Fridays to cover the overlap between business travel, weekend leisure travel and the beginning of the weekend ski traffic. Normal Fridays are not as busy as this, however. With very little business travel on Saturdays and Sundays, 91 and 99 units are sufficient, reverting to a more normal workload of 79 on Monday. The 100 or so trainsets in service is PSE's maximum effort, achieved by a combination of concentrating maintenance in the Tuesday to Thursday period, scheduling major refurbishments at Bischheim outside this period, and modifying platform workings at the Gare-de-Lyon to achieve short turnarounds with in-and-out working.

SUD-EST FLEET DEPLOYMENT										
	Tues-Thurs		Friday		Saturday		Sunday		Monday	
Fleet	Units	Avge Daily km	Units	Avge Daily km	Units	Avge Daily km	Units	Avge Daily km	Units	Avge Daily km
First Class	6	1,440	6	1,321	4	1,017	3	1,038	6	1,224
Two Class:Three Voltage 'Swiss'	5	1,420	7	1,370	6	1,179	7	1,066	6	1,263
Two Class: Two Voltage	59	1,301	79	1,231	81	1,248	82	1,205	60	1,278
Atlantique	6	1,409	9	1,166	14*	1,199	11	1,340	7	1,360
Total Units In Service	76		101		91		99		79	
* Plus 14 extra sets on February Saturdays										

The above table shows the number of trainsets required to provide the service on the appropriate days of the week, together with the average daily kilometres per unit. A summary of the total day-by-day fleet kilometreage is shown below. It should be noted that these figures are trainset kilometres and not train kilometres; a service which has a single unit on Thursdays which is doubled on Fridays achieves the same train kilometreage but trainset kilometres are of course double. Nevertheless, the difference between Tuesday and Thursday is quite dramatic – 25 extra trainsets in service achieving a fleet total of 125,232 kilometres.

As they were built to provide a concentrated number of First Class seats on peak business trains, the six First Class sets work exclusively between Paris and Lyon, sometimes making as many as four single trips in a day. Before the Grenoble service was separated from the Lyon service, one First Class trainset used to make a return trip between Grenoble and Paris. These sets tend to be under-utilised at weekends, but sometimes work a Saturday/Sunday return trip from Paris to Nice and back; one set works between Paris and Bourg-St-Maurice on a Saturday Ski special.

PARIS SUD EST: WEEKLY KILOMETRES					
Fleet	Tuesday Wednesday Thursday	Friday	Saturday	Sunday	Monday
First Class	8,640	7,925	4,065	3,114	7,344
Two Class: 3-Voltage 'Swiss'	7,100	9,587	7,074	7,460	7,578
Two Class: 2-Voltage	76,735	97,226	83,608	93,982	76,662
Atlantique	8,451	10,494	16,778	14,734	9,514
TOTAL	100,926	125,232	111,525	119,290	101,098
Tues, Wed, Thurs	302,778				
Friday	125,232				
Saturday	111,525				
Sunday	119,290				
Monday	101,098				
TOTAL	759,923				

For most of the time the small 'Swiss' sub-fleet works the four daily through services to Lausanne and the single trip to Bern. To provide some flexibility they also cover a single journey to Chalon-sur-Saône and Besançon which are part of the same train service group built on the Paris-Dijon axis.

The number of Atlantique sets working on the PSE varies, and to some extent is dependent on driver knowledge and the ratio of First to Second Class passengers. As they must normally work as single units they are placed on services with lighter traffic, but with 10 as opposed to eight trailers they do offer an additional 100 or so seats compared with the standard PSE set. Atlantique sets currently work to Dijon, Lyon, Annecy, Grenoble, Marseille and Nice. They also cover a number of special services to the ski resorts during the winter programme.

The fleet of two-class two-voltage trainsets are the workhorses of the Sud Est network. Particular mention should be made of the service between Lyon and Lille/Rouen. For part of the year this consists of two separate trains from Lille and Rouen direct to Lyon, but in the off-peak period the two services combine at Valenton in the outskirts of Paris to go forward as one service from there to Lyon. The northbound working also varies. During the summer there is a second service in each direction between Lyon and Lille.

Some PSE train working highlights are shown in the table below which details 13 workings of particular interest. Whilst the 1 hour 30 minutes timing from Paris to Mâcon-Loché is the fastest time – *Vitesse Commerciale* 220.2 km/h (136.8 mph) – the benchmark timing is the flat 2 hours between Paris and Lyon Part-Dieu. Both in terms of speed and frequency, this is the 'flagship' service on the core route. But not every train gets the 2 hours timing. Where operating margins are tight on busy sections of route in the Paris and Lyon area, up to four extra minutes is allowed at certain times of the day in some cases. This also provides a reserve should the 'white period' be exceeded or for other examples of unforeseen delays. An extra four minutes in the Paris to Lyon timing is the equivalent of one train path per hour; SNCF plans to dispense with this and standardise all trains at 2 hours in the future.

Very long non-stop journeys are an important timetable feature. These are made possible by the system of train crew working arrangements. Staff work to a point up to the maximum permitted hours within a shift of duty where they sign off and rest in one of the hostels provided by the SNCF at strategic points

PARIS SUD EST: OPERATING HIGHLIGHTS						
Journey sector	Distance		Time		Average speed	
	Km	Miles	Hr	Min	km/h	mph
Paris: Mâcon-Loché	363.4	225.8	1	39	220.2	136.8
Paris: Lyon Part-Dieu	427.9	265.9	2	00	213.9	132.9
Paris: Le Creusot	303.2	188.4	1	26	211.5	131.4
Paris: Bourg-en-Bresse	402.9	250.4	1	55	210.2	130.6
Paris: Grenoble	553.7	344.0	2	55	190.0	118.0
Paris: Valence	534.0	331.8	2	53	185.2	115.0
Paris: Chambéry (1)	530.0	329.3	2	54	182.8	113.6
Paris: Dijon	284.7	176.9	1	37	176.1	109.4
Paris: Avignon	658.4	409.1	3	45	175.6	109.1
Paris: Bellegarde	515.8	320.5	3	00	172.0	106.9
Longeau: Lyon Part-Dieu	566.0	351.7	3	21	169.0	105.0
Paris: Annemasse (2)	554.8	344.8	3	38	152.7	94.9
Lyon Part-Dieu: Toulon	416.0	258.5	3	10	131.4	81.6

(1) Via Lyon Contournement and St-André-le-Gaz
(2) Operates on limited days in Ski season

throughout the network. These arrangements are known as *repos hors résidence* or rest away from home. Because of the size of the SNCF network, French drivers have a far more extensive route knowledge than their contemporaries on other European railways. Each driver is required to sign that he has knowledge – location of stations, points, signals, gradients, other specific features etc – over the routes he is required to work. Paris-based drivers routinely work to Dijon, Besançon the Swiss border town at Vallorbe, Geneva, Chambéry, Saint Gervais, Grenoble, Lyon, Montpellier, Marseille and Lille. Other depots covering Sud Est TGV work are Dijon, Lyon, Chambéry, Nîmes, Marseille, Lille and Rouen. With the introduction of cross-country TGVs from Tours, Nantes and Rennes, drivers from Rennes also work through to Lyon; Lyon crews work similarly to Rennes, Tours and Poitiers. Given the combination of work practices and route knowledge, the Sud Est has a number of interesting long non-stop runs daily. They include:

Paris-Avignon: 658.4 km (409.1 miles)
Three northbound and two southbound TGVs are scheduled to make this run daily. The main challenge is preventing delay from other services, particularly through the Lyon area.

Longeau-Lyon Part-Dieu: 566 km (351.7 miles)
This working – performed by Paris or Lille drivers – involves knowledge of the Nord region between Lille and the outskirts of Paris as well as the 'Grande Centure' lines to the east of Paris. However, from 1994, these trains will probably be transferred to the Le Jonction route. Nonetheless this is a very complicated itinerary to work, particularly the tortuous passage of the Grande Centure lines.

Paris-Annemasse: 554.8 km (344.8 miles)
Extensive route knowledge is put to good use during the ski season from January through to the end of April when many special trains run direct to the winter sports stations. A weekend service from Paris to St Gervais in Haute Savoie shows what can be achieved. St Gervais is at the end of a single line branch reached by way of the Bellegarde–Evian line and then from Annemasse to La Roche-sur-Foron. Paris to Bellegarde, en route to Geneva, is a normal TGV journey. In this case the train runs directly through Bellegarde and on to the Evian branch to make its first stop at Annemasse, a distance of 554.8 km from Paris.

ATLANTIQUE

While the same basic principles apply to the Atlantique operations, the characteristics of the service are quite different from Paris-Sud Est. The most important difference is that there is no core traffic flow equal in volume or intensity to that between Paris and Lyon. The populations of the largest centres on the network are relatively small – Le Mans has 145,502 inhabitants, Rennes 197,536, Nantes 244,995, Tours 125,509 and Bordeaux 210,336. As the Atlantique network serves a large number of popular holiday resorts, the market tends to be motivated more by leisure rather than business travel.

Technical differences are also important. While the route kilometreage is less than the PSE, the high speed route starts only 5 km from Paris Montparnasse station and – with a maximum speed of 300 rather than 270 km/h – some very fast journey times are achieved but over shorter distances. Another interesting feature is the upgrading of sections of classic route so that TGVs continue to run at quite high speeds, up to 220 km/h, to reach their final destination. They are: 20 or so km from the end of the Brittany branch at Connerré to the approaches to Le Mans station; most of the 185 km from Le Mans to Nantes and a significant part of the route from Monts Junction (south of Tours) to Bordeaux. This latter part of the Paris-Bordeaux classic route – which is electrified at 1.5 kV dc – was upgraded during the 1970s so that locomotive-hauled trains could run at 200 km/h. The line speed was subsequently raised to 220 km/h for TGVs.

To provide sufficient seating capacity or to offer a service to two separate destinations, all TGVs (but not the Eurostar derivative) can run with two units coupled in multiple. Two units are coupled with the Scharfenberg automatic coupler locked in position.
Brian Perren

Some services from Marseille and Montpellier combine or divide at Avignon from where they run non-stop to Paris. A two-unit formation pulls away from Avignon station for its 409-mile non-stop run to Paris.
Brian Perren

Below: **There is space in vehicle R1 in Atlantique sets for luggage.**
Brian Perren

Point-to-point running times for the Atlantique line – see tables below and opposite – produce some very fast journeys. On the South Western ('Aquitaine') branch the running time for the 225.5 km from the start of the LGV at Montrouge-Châtillon to its end at Monts Junction is 56 minutes – an average speed of 241.6 km/h (150 mph). The time from Montrouge-Châtillon to the end of the Britanny branch is 46 minutes – an average speed of 227.5 km/h (141.3 mph). These times produce journeys of 56 minutes from Paris Montparnasse to St-Pierre-des-Corps (Tours) (average speed 236.6 km/h: 147 mph) and 53 minutes to Le Mans (average speed 226.1 km/h: 140.5 mph). The fastest time on the line – indeed the fastest time in the world – is 50½ minutes from Massy TGV station to St-Pierre-des-Corps; average speed 245.8 km/h (152.7 mph). The time from Paris Montparnasse to the TGV station at Vendôme is also very fast – average speed 230.9 km/h (143.4 mph).

Running at 300 km/h on the LGV is of course very satisfactory, but the speeds now achieved over upgraded classic routes are also significant. The fastest time over the 568 km (353 miles) from Paris Montparnasse to Bordeaux is 2 hours 54 minutes, calling for an average speed of 196 km/h (121.8 mph). The timing from Paris Montparnasse to Monts Junction is, as mentioned, 56 minutes, leaving 118 minutes for the remaining 337 km (209 miles) over classic tracks to Bordeaux. This calls for an average speed of 171.4 km/h (106 mph) over a route with 18 variations in maximum line speed and equipped with dc power supplies.

There are 56 basic services in each direction over the Atlantique LGV, but many of these are two-unit services which divide/combine to serve different destinations. A number of services divide at Rennes into separate trains for Brest or Quimper. Similarly at Bordeaux, trains divide into sections for Toulouse, Dax and Irun. In some cases a unit may be added to provide sufficient seating over the main section of the route between Paris and Bordeaux, Paris and Nantes or Paris and Rennes.

With only two intermediate stations, a single fleet of trains with identical power, weight and performance characteristics able to run at equal speeds, timetabling the Atlantique service should – on the face of things – be a relatively simple task. As the new line only covers 278 route kilometres covered in less than 1 hour, the Atlantique trains spend a greater proportion of their time running over conventional routes used also by other trains, including rural stopping services and to a lesser extent freights.

ATLANTIQUE SCHEDULE: PARIS MONTPARNASSE/COURTALAIN-LE MANS (1)			
	km Points	Cumulative point-to-point times (mins)	Cumulative km
PRS 17 Bifurcation Courtalain	130.4	33	130
PRS 31 Le Plessis	149.6	38	150
PRS 32 Dollon	172.8	44	173
Le Parc Sub Station	179.6	46	180
End of LGV	180.4	-	-
Montfort Le Gesnois	193.9	47	185
Yure L'Eveque	204.1	50	195
Le Mans station	211.0	54	202

Paris Montparnasse-Le Mans 54 Min
Average speed: 224.4 km/h (139.5 mph)

(1) Timing and distance data from Montparnasse to Bifurcation Courtalain are shown opposite

ATLANTIQUE SCHEDULE:
PARIS MONTPARNASSE-BORDEAUX ST JEAN

	Km Points	Cumulative point to point times (mins)	Cumulative km
Paris Montparnasse	-	-	-
Montrouge-Châtillon	6.0	4	6
PRS 11 Massy TGV	13.7	6	14
PRS 12 Marcoussis	25.3	9	25
PRS 13 St Arnoult	44.6	14	45
PRS 14 St Leger	67.4	21	67
PRS 15 Rouvray	92.2	24	92
PRS 16 Dangeau	114.0	29	114
PRS 17 Bifurfaction Courtalain	130.4	33	130
PRS 41 Drove	138.2	34	138
Vendôme TGV station	162.0	40	162
PRS 43 St Amand	178.6	43	178
PRS 44 St Cyr	188.2	45	188
PRS 45 Loire	215.2	51	215
Monts km 231.5 LGV (1)	246.8	56	231
Port De Piles	281.1	65	265
Dange	289.2	68	273
Châtellerault	303.5	73	287
Jaunay Clan	324.6	80	308
Poitiers	336.5	85	320
Couhe Verac	370.0	96	354
St Soviol	388.0	102	372
Ruffec	402.1	106	386
Luxe	420.3	113	404
Angoulême	449.3	125	432
Montmoreau	483.4	138	467
Chalais	499.9	143	484
Coutras	531.1	152	515
Libourne	547.0	158	531
St Loubes	565.0	165	549
Bordeaux St Jean	583.5	174	568

Paris Montparnasse-Bordeaux St Jean 174 min
Average speed: 195.9 km/h (121.7 mph)

(1) Km 231.5 is the end of the LGV where it joins the classic route to Bordeaux
at km 246.8

TGV ATLANTIQUE: OPERATING HIGHLIGHTS

Journey sector	Distance		Time		Average speed	
	Km	Miles	Hr	Min	km/h	mph
Massy TGV: St-Pierre-des-Corps	206.9	128.6	0	50½	245.8	152.7
Paris Montparnasse: St-Pierre-des-Corps	220.8	137.2	0	56	236.6	147.0
Paris Montparnasse: Vendôme	161.6	100.4	0	42	230.9	143.4
Paris Montparnasse: Le Mans	201.6	125.3	0	53½	226.1	140.5
Paris Montparnasse: Nantes	385.7	239.7	1	59½	193.7	120.3
Paris Montparnasse: Rennes	363.8	226.1	2	02	178.9	111.2
Paris Montparnasse: Poitiers	320.9	199.4	1	30	213.9	132.9
Paris Montparnasse: Bordeaux	568.3	353.1	2	54	196.0	121.8

Among the factors influencing the design of the Atlantique train service are Montparnasse station at Paris and the 337 km (209 miles) of route from the point where the new line joins the existing two-track route to Bordeaux at Monts Junction south of Tours. Paris Montparnasse has 24 main platforms plus a further four (25 to 28) at Vaugirard. There are four dedicated TGV tracks – TGV 1, TGV 2bis and TGV 2 are the main running lines which merge into two tracks further out while tracks M1 and M2 are the access lines to Châtillon TGV depot; all of these lines are signalled for reversible working. There are four tracks towards Versailles, paired by direction. The normal working for TGVs is to route incoming trains on track TGV 2 over the flyover into the western side of the layout (platforms 13 to 24); after detraining passengers the set will then be worked out to Châtillon Depot using track M1.

All TGVs are rostered to visit Châtillon Depot for cleaning and maintenance at least once every 24 hours; depending on the roster, a unit would return to service within 1 hour using tracks M1 or M2 to reach the eastern side of the station (platforms 3 to 12) to take up its outward working. On Fridays, when the service is considerably increased, some incoming trains are routed directly into platforms 2 to 12 where they will form an outward service after servicing. Part of the track layout in the station area and out to Châtillon Depot has been redesigned; the flow of trains in and out must be reasonably evenly spread. This determines the time of trains coming on to the new line at Monts, Montlouis or Connerré and in turn has timing implications over the entire Atlantique network.

Left: **Line up at Châtillon Depot**. GEC Alsthom

Below: **The servicing sidings at Châtillon Depot.** SNCF

The second major factor is the pathing of trains between Monts Junction and Bordeaux St Jean station. While upgrading has enabled TGVs to travel from Monts to Bordeaux in around 2 hours (average speed 109 mph), the need to operate with two block sections reduces line capacity. Fitting in local services can therefore be difficult.

Atlantique trainset utilisation is shown below. As is the case with the PSE fleet, the maximum turnout is on Fridays with 79 sets in service and this is also sustained on Saturdays and Sundays. The total weekly fleet kilometreage is 547,910.

TGV ATLANTIQUE FLEET KILOMETRES		
	kms	Trainsets in Service
Tuesday	73,359	58
Wednesday	73,359	58
Thursday	73,359	58
Friday	101,234	79
Saturday	61,619	77
Sunday	80,767	79
Monday	84,213	79
	547,910	
Includes five sets working cross-country services from Atlantique stations to Lyon, but excludes units working on PSE services		

Traffic control and supervision

Thanks to the quality of its engineering and dedication of its staff, SNCF has been able to maintain a very high standard of operating performance throughout the TGV network. By themselves, engineering excellence and a robust timetable plan are not enough to ensure consistent standards of performance. Thus, there is a need for an organisation which will supervise operations on a day-to-day basis so that the work of all departments who contribute to the business is properly co-ordinated.

Like all other railways, SNCF had in place a fully-developed traffic control organisation well before TGV was built. This organisation is geographically based and works through a network of control centres located in the regional offices such as Dijon, Lyon and Marseille. This organisation – which still exists – has worked very well, but as the characteristics of the new TGV service are so very different from conventional flows of passenger and freight traffic, SNCF felt that it would be advantageous to concentrate all information, control and supervision in one specific purpose-built centre for the Paris Sud Est line.

There are now three such centres – for the Sud Est located near the Gare-de-Lyon, for the Atlantique located in the Montparnasse station complex adjoining the new station signalling centre and at Lille for TGV Nord Europe. As well as supervising domestic traffic, the Lille centre – which opened in May 1993 – will also be the focal point for the Eurostar and PBKA international services.

Basically these control centres are responsible for the 24 hour supervision of all TGV operations – train running, monitoring of loadings, modifications to schedules, and the maintenance of track, power supplies and signalling. In other words its function is to ensure that the trains run to time, that customer demand is met by providing extra capacity where necessary and that maximum revenue earning potential is achieved by utilising the yield management system to ensure good load factors on each train.

There are four separate activities, and all the controllers working in the centre are located together for easy contact:

Traffic and energy control

This section is responsible for traffic control, achieved by means of permanent radio links with the drivers on the trains, supported by computerised information systems, for resolving any operational difficulties which may arise and for taking such steps as necessary to minimise disruptions to the service. They also control and monitor the supply of power from the sub-stations to the catenary.

Operations control

Essentially the task of the operations control group is to supervise the work and disposition of the TGV fleet. Although the workings of individual units are pre-arranged in advance by the production department, unforeseen circumstances often make it necessary to modify a unit-working at very short notice. For example, a small defect may detain a unit in the depot beyond the scheduled maintenance time and another train has to be positioned to take its place. Late running, or unit failure en route, may also make it necessary to adjust rosters and position a replacement train. Operational control is carried out by close and constant contact with the two main Paris maintenance installations – Bercy Conflans and Villeneuve (AMPSE) workshops, together with the locations in the provinces – plus Geneva, Lausanne and Bern, where TGVs are stabled overnight.

An interesting feature of TGV operations and marketing is the flexibility built into the system whereby units and crew can be organised at reasonably short notice to provide a relief service. While known peak traffic days – Fridays throughout the year, holiday peaks and public holidays – can be provided for in advance, special events may generate additional traffic at short notice. In this regard the work of this unit involves monitoring the computer seat reservation system to see if a particular service is booking heavily at specific times in advance. At a given loading ratio it may be decided to strengthen the train from a single to a two-unit formation or provide a complete duplicate service. Provision of the extra unit may involve a positioning trip on a scheduled service to a provincial centre or an arrangement to work the additional unit back to Paris as soon as possible. Train crews and catering also have to be organised. If a single-unit service becomes a two-unit service, an additional catering crew and ticket controllers are of course necessary.

Programme control
This section compiles schedules for track maintenance work and monitors these in liaison with the appropriate engineering departments.

The despatching and signalling centre (PAR)
The nerve centre for carrying out all operating functions is the *Poste d'Aiguillage de Régulation* (PAR) or Despatch and Signalling Centre. PAR combines the role of a signalling and traffic control and its control area coincides with the new railway. On the PSE its outer limits are at Lieusaint, Aisy, Pont-de-Veyle and Sathonay. On the Atlantique line the area extends from Montrouge-Châtillon to Connerré and Monts Junction. Trains are passed to or received from the new line by contact between PAR and the neighbouring conventional signal boxes. PAR operates – by means of four computerised, electronic-based systems – for the monitoring of signalling installations and traction current supply; the track diagrams and control panels for signalling and energy supplies together with the operator's control desk and corresponding circuits; computerised train describer and route control systems; and a central hot-axlebox detection system. This operates by means of an infra-red detector device which gives the temperature of all axleboxes and records various measurements as trains pass.

By their very nature, all transport systems – air, road or rail – are liable to delay through unforeseen or extraneous circumstances. How emergency arrangements are made and implemented to restore traffic to normal is a reflection on the management system and the quality of back-up.

While the rate of failure in service is very low, trains sometimes fail. If the failure is on the TGV line itself, the following options may be exercised. As all TGV lines are signalled for bidirectional working at full line speed, following trains will be diverted to run on the other track to avoid the defective train, and resuming their normal itinerary at the next crossover. This will of course involve stopping or curtailing trains in the opposite direction. If it is a bad failure to the extent that the train cannot be moved under its own power, it may be necessary for it to be pushed by the following service into one of the 'refuge' loops located along the line. These are at Marolles, Vaumort, La Cour-D'Arcenay, Montchanin and Mâcon. At Montchanin and Mâcon the length of the station platforms is extended by an extra 400 metres so that passengers can be transferred from a defective two-unit service to a replacement one.

In addition, Marolles, Vaumort, La Cour-D'Arcenay are 'ghost stations', equipped with 800 metre platforms, the purpose of which is to provide a place for emergency evacuation of a failed train. There are similar facilities at Saint Leger, Dangeau and Dollon on the Atlantique line. On Nord Europe they are located at Fresnoy (Pk 39), Gare Picarde (Pk 110), Beugnatre (Pk 143), Oignies (Pk 182), Wannehain (Pk 208) and Hondeghen. Emergency facilities – at Satolas station and at Claveyson-Bren (Pk 476) between Satolas and Valence – will be provided on the Lyon Contournement.

An important contribution to reliability is the positioning of spare trainsets and relief crews. As mentioned earlier, there is a reserve in the work programmes to cover such contingencies. For example, if a train from the provinces into Paris is badly delayed and cannot complete its full roster, a relief unit will be pressed into service from the sidings to cover the outward departure. Similarly, if a train fails en route a reserve train can be despatched to provide relief. Generally speaking, there are reserve drivers to cope with these situations, able to take over a train for a long run should this be necessary at relatively short notice.

15. SNCF: Master Plan

With the proven success of the routes now in public service in France and routes currently being constructed, the time for a more ambitious stage has been reached. Accordingly, in January 1989, the French Government asked SNCF to prepare a master plan for a national network of high-speed rail routes in France. There are two aspects to this plan – the French domestic and the wider European dimension.

So far as France itself is concerned, there is the need to find a means of containing the growing levels of motorway and air traffic congestion; to seek a means of protecting the environment and to provide for the rational use of land space and to improve transport links between the French regions for economic and social purposes. This can be achieved by extending the TGV network beyond the 1,246 km of route now in service or being constructed.

Equally important – not only for France but for the whole of the European Community – is the need to plan the French TGV network with due regard to the plans of neighbouring countries. Projects, in hand or planned, in neighbouring countries include:

Germany

◆ 427 km of route now in service between Hannover and Wurzburg and between Mannheim and Stuttgart
◆ The Cologne to Frankfurt project – the key route in the DB network
◆ Upgrading the existing main line between Karlsruhe and Bale to be completed in 1994
◆ 260 km project from Hannover to Berlin

Italy

◆ The Rome–Florence line (260 km) now in service
◆ Florence–Milan (285 km)
◆ Rome–Naples–Battipaglia (296 km)
◆ Venice–Turin (411 km)

Spain

◆ Madrid–Seville (476 km) commissioned in 1992
◆ Madrid to Barcelona – in the planning stage
◆ Barcelona to the French border at Le Perthus

These and other projects have been documented in a plan presented in December 1990 by the EC Commission to the European Council of transport ministers. In total the EC plan could cover 30,000 km of lines including 9,000 km of new routes, 15,000 km of existing routes upgraded for 200 km/h and 1,200 km of existing lines which would provide access between various routes.

The routes set out in the SNCF master plan (see map overleaf) – which complements the wider European plan – will be integrated into the existing classic network. In some cases existing conventional routes will be upgraded for higher speeds.

PROJET DE SCHEMA DIRECTEUR NATIONAL
DES LIAISONS FERROVIAIRES A GRANDE VITESSE

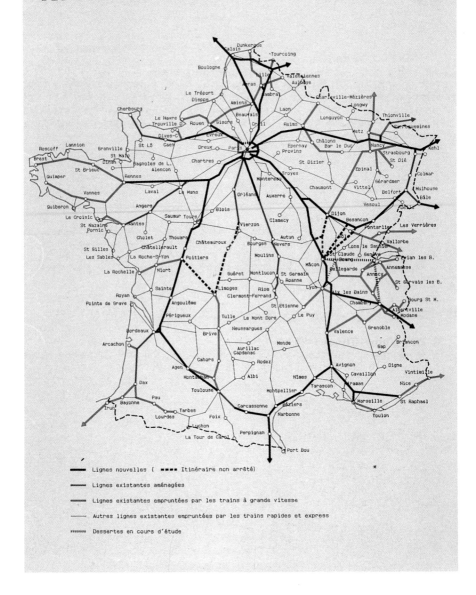

Lignes nouvelles (▪▪▪▪ Itinéraire non arrêté)

Lignes existantes aménagées

Lignes existantes empruntées par les trains à grande vitesse

Autres lignes existantes empruntées par les trains rapides et express

Dessertes en cours d'étude

There are eight major projects:

1. South European TGV

This 647 km (402 miles) of route is an extension of the PSE line (Rhône Alpes extension) southwards from Valence to a point near Avignon where it will split into two branches – one towards Marseille and the Côte D'Azur and the other towards Montpellier and Barcelona. There has been controversy over the precise choice of route through Provence. At the time of writing, the public enquiry in preparation for the 'Declaration of Public Utility' by the Government is completed for the section of route from Valence to Marseille/Montpellier. Studies will begin soon for the extension from Montpellier to the Spanish Border.

2. TGV Est (460 km)

This will run eastwards from Paris to Strasbourg and into Germany where it will link up with the DB high-speed network. The basic characteristics of the route have been approved by the French and German governments. However, the precise alignment and the financing are still under study. A decision to build the first stage from Paris to Baudrécourt about 15 km beyond Metz on the line to Sarrebourg was announced on 31 December 1992.

3. TGV Aquitaine and Midi Pyrenees (538 km)

Extension of TGV Atlantique from south of Tours to the South West of France and linking up with Spain and Portugal.

4. Trans-Alpine (252 km)

Starting near Lyon this line will connect the French and Italian high-speed networks through a 50 km deep-level base tunnel. This route will carry traffic from Britain and Benelux in the north and from Spain and Portugal in the south. Initial studies have been approved by the French and Italian governments.

5. Jonction-Sud (49 km)

High-speed line to link the Atlantique and Sud Est lines in the Ile-de-France.

6. TGV Rhine–Rhône (425 km)

In combination with the South European TGV, this route will provide a link between Germany, Eastern France, Southern France and Spain.

7. TGV Brittany (156 km)

Extension of western branch of TGV Atlantique.

8. TGV Grand Sud (700 km)

This cross country link will include the major cities in Southern France – Bordeaux, Toulouse, Montpellier, Marseille and Nice – as well as providing a link into Spain from Toulouse.

Totalling some 3,430 km of additional new high-speed infrastructure, the master plan would be implemented over a period of 10 to 20 years. Its likely order of cost is FFr 180 billion for infrastructure plus FFr 30 billion for a further 340 trains. The pace at which this plan proceeds will depend on a number of factors – the rate of return for each project, the willingness of local authorities to make a financial contribution to projects where the rate of return is not sufficiently high and availability of finance in the light of competing national projects.

16. TGV for the World

Given its accumulated experience in the design, construction, operating and marketing of rail services at speeds over 250 km/h, other countries have been looking to SNCF and the French railway industry for technical assistance and expertise.

In the post-war years, France had already become established as a major exporter of railway equipment and expertise. To cope with the growing number of consultancy enquiries and management projects, SNCF created a subsidiary to organise and handle this business. Established in 1957, *Société Française D'Etudes Et De Réalisations Ferroviaires* (SOFRERAIL) is today the railway subsidiary of Systra, a holding company whose shareholders are SNCF, RATP (the Paris Transport Authority) plus a number of leading French banks.

This corporate structure ensures that SOFRERAIL is independent of any individual manufacturer or equipment supplier. SOFRERAIL offers an range of services all of which are related to rail expertise or technology – operating, marketing and design, technical assistance and training. The company has a permanent staff of 300, which is strengthened on an ad hoc basis by experts from SNCF who undertake specific short-term specialist assignments. Typically 80,000 work hours per year are undertaken in SNCF design offices.

TGV technology has already been chosen for the Trans Manche and PBKA joint-European projects where France is directly involved, but also for the high-speed line between Madrid and Seville (the AVE) which opened for service in 1992. Beyond Europe SOFRERAIL is involved in various projects including a scheme in Taiwan for a new railway between Taipei and Kaohsiung, a similar project in North Korea for a railway between Seoul and Pusan, and the Texas Supertrain project in the United States

AVE (Alta Velocidad Espanola)

During the past 10 or so years the economy of Spain has been flourishing to the extent that the Spanish Government has been giving attention to improving transportation links both within Spain and with the rest of Europe. In 1986 the Spanish Government decided to sponsor a new high-speed railway over 471 km (293 miles), linking Madrid in the north and Seville in the south with intermediate stations to serve Ciudad Real, Puertollano, Cordaba, Seville (Santa Justa) and a station to serve the site of the 1992 Seville Expo.

Before work could start it was necessary to address the critical issue of track width – for the railways of Spain were built with a spacing of 1.668 metres between rails whereas the rest of mainland Europe, plus Britain but not Ireland, has a width of 1.435 metres. While it has been possible to design rolling stock which can be adapted at border stations to run out of Spain to points in Europe, the conversion process takes about 20 or so minutes and the trains require special maintenance.

Partly because the characteristics of the new Spanish line would preclude anything other than high-speed trains, but also because Spain could see a long-term benefit by joining the European High Speed network, it was decided to build the AVE to the standard 1.435-metre width between rails. Spain envisages an extension of the AVE from Madrid to Barcelona to link up with the French and beyond that the European system.

As can be seen from this picture, the Spanish AVE trainsets are identical to the SNCF Atlantique sets. Renfe

The new line – which opened for business on 20 April 1991 – has 31 viaducts totalling 9.8 km and 17 tunnels totalling 15.8 km. The ruling gradient is 1.25% and the operating speed is 250 km/h, except in tunnels where it is 200 km/h, although the line has been designed for a maximum speed of 300 km/h.

Rather than develop a new design, RENFE decided to use a proven product and opted to purchase 16 trains from GEC Alsthom based on the TGV Atlantique design. These trains – which were partly built in France and partly in Spain – have two power cars and eight trailers: power is 8,800 kW, the maximum speed 300 km/h, length is 200 metres and weight is 421.5 tonnes. The line is wired for 25 kV but the trains are also equipped for 3 kV dc to facilitate the distribution system in the main stations where the terminals are shared with existing RENFE lines. Internal configuration – with a total of 329 seats – has been modified for RENFE's needs. Journey times between Madrid and Seville are 2 hours 45 minutes to 2 hours 55 minutes.

Taiwan

Outline plans for the Taipei-Kaohsiung high-speed rail link are well advanced, but no firm decision to go-ahead has been taken. SOFRERAIL was engaged to undertake preliminary planning studies, although the building of the line and the supply of the trains could be awarded either to France, Germany or Japan. The length of the line is 350 km (217 miles) and the anticipated maximum speed is 350 km/h. Commissioning of the line is targeted for 1999 and by 2011 between 60 and 70 million passengers per year are expected. Estimated cost is around US $15 billion. The tender for the basic system – trains, signalling, overhead catenary equipment – is expected in mid-1994.

South Korea

SOFRERAIL produced a feasibility study for a 411 km high-speed line between Seoul and Pusan. In August 1993, in face of intense competition from Japan and Germany, a consortium led by GEC ALSTHOM was awarded the contract to provide the technology and supply the trains. There will be 46 TGV trainsets formed with two power cars and 18 trailers seating 1,038 passengers. Motor bogie configuration will be similar to SNCF PSE and Eurostar (TMST) sets; operating speed is 300 km/h. CSEE Transport will instal TVM 430. SOFRERAIL will assist with training of Korean personnel. About half of the equipment will be manufactured in Korea. Target date for completion is 1999; 80 million passengers a year are expected to use the line in the first five years. South Korea is the first country outside Europe to adopt the TGV system.

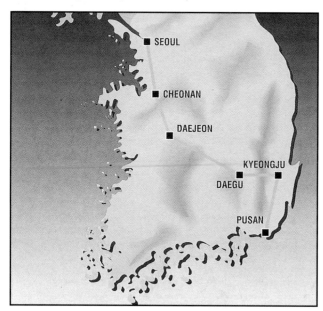

Map of the Seoul – Pusan TGV route.

The South Korean trains will have 18 trailers between their two power cars. GEC Alsthom

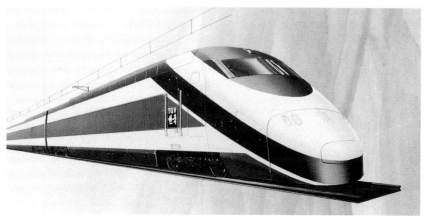

Texas Supertrain

In May 1991 the Texas TGV consortium, which is headed by the Morrison Knudsen Corporation, was awarded the franchise to design, build and operate a high-speed rail system in the state of Texas. Impressed by the success of TGV in France, a group of Texan businessmen saw the potential that a high-speed rail link could solve the growing problems of air and road traffic congestion in the Texas triangle formed by Dallas-Fort Worth in the north, San Antonio in the south and Houston in the south east.

The prospects for the new railway – now branded Texas Supertrain – are very good. It will link the State's three prime business centres and areas of population with stations in city centres, at convenient suburban railheads and links to Dallas-Fort Worth and Houston airports. Travel by all modes in Texas was around 19 million in 1988 and is expected to rise to 30 million by 1998 and 60 million by 2015. By the year 2000 a total of 8.7 million rail journeys per year will be made by the new Texas Supertrain rising to 14.5 million by 2015. Estimated cost of the project – which will be funded entirely by private venture capital without any state or government subsidy – is around US $6.8 billion.

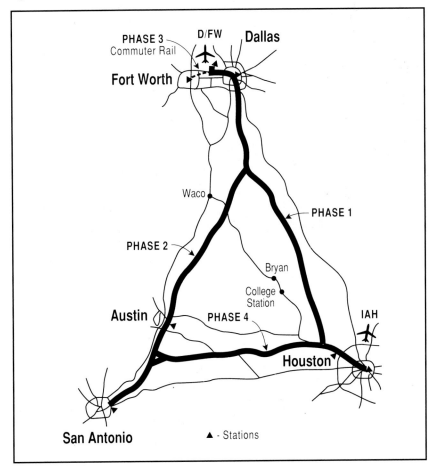

The network will be developed in four stages and the first stage will be the eastern leg of the triangle from Houston to Dallas-Fort Worth airport. A year later this will be followed by the second stage comprising the western leg from San Antonio through Austin to join the eastern leg to Dallas. Stage three, which is currently under discussion, is the development of a commuter corridor between Dallas, Fort Worth and Dallas-Fort Worth airports. Together with regional and municipal authorities, Texas TGV is developing a case to proceed with this aspect of the project.

Stage four – the base of the triangle from Houston to Austin and San Antonio – would complete the project. Capital costs at 1990 values are US $2,502 million for stage one and US $1,718 million for stage two. Implementation of the project beyond the US $ 42,220 million for stages one and two is limited by the capacity of the private capital markets. On present time scales stage one should be open in July 1998 followed by stage two in March 1999.

A total of 33 trainsets will be required to work the service. These will incorporate GEC Alsthom TGV technology and will be assembled in the United States by Bombardier, the North American manufacturer of TGV trainsets. Final design details have not yet been completed, but the trains will consist of two power cars and eight articulated trailers.

The Texas triangle is an ideal location for a high-speed rail system. With an operating speed of 320 km/h and a limited number of intermediate stops, journey times between the main centres are well below the threshold where journeys by air begin to become more effective than rail. It will only take 1 hour 30 minutes to travel from the centre of Dallas to the Central Business District in Houston; similar journey time from Dallas to San Antonio is only 1 hour 44 minutes. Each route will have a service frequency of 30 minutes, increased to 15 minutes during peak periods, and will operate from 0600 to 2300. There will be 32 return journeys on each leg.

With the exception of the Amtrak North East Corridor service from Washington DC through New York to Boston which operates at 120 mph, there is no other inter-city service in the United States. Texas Supertrain is an interesting development and may well pave the way for further projects in the USA

Australia

The Australian government is considering a proposal from GEC Alsthom for a high speed train project between Sydney and Canberra.

Canada

The Canadian High Speed Train project was announced by Bombardier in February 1990. If it goes ahead the cities of Quebec, Montreal, Ottawa, Toronto and Windsor will be served by a 1215 km rail link at speeds up to 300 km/h. Operation would be shared between Canadian National and Canadian Pacific.

SUMMARY OF TGV AND DERIVATIVE TRAINSETS

	Built/ delivered	No of units	Vehicle formation PC	FC	SC	CS (1)	Total	Seating FC	SC	Total	Length Metres	Masse Tonnes	Max speed Km/h	25 kv	15 kv	3 kv	1.5 kv	750	Traction Motors/ Output Kw (2)	Bogies M	T	Notes
Paris Sud Est																						
Two Class	1978-85	91	2	3	5	-	10	108	260	368	200.19	385	270	✓			✓		12x535 =6420	6	7	
First Class	1981-84	9	2	8	-	-	10	285	-	285	200.19	379	270	✓			✓			6	7	
Three volt: Swiss	1981-85	9	2	3	5	-	10	108	260	368	200.19	394	270	✓			✓			6	7	
Postal	1984	2½	2	-	-	-	10	-	-	-	200.19	345	270	✓			✓			6	8	3
Total		111½																				
Atlantique	1989-92	105	2	3	6	1	12	116	369	485	237.59	484	300	✓			✓		8x1100 =8800	4	11	
Eurostar (TMST)	1993-95	31	2	6	10	2	20	210	584	794	393.72	800	300	✓		✓		✓	12x1166 =14000	6	18	4
Eurostar (TMST) North of London	1994-95	7	2	4	8	2	16	114	464	578	318.92	600	300	✓		✓		✓	12x1166 =14000	6	16	5
AVE	1991-92	16	2	3	4	1	10	116	213	329	200.19	392	220	✓		✓			8x1100 =8800	4	9	6, 7
Réseau: TGV R																						
Two voltage	1992-94	50	2	3	4	-	10	120	257	377	200.19	383	300	✓					8x1100 =8800	4	9	
Three voltage	1993-95	40	2	3	5	-	10	120	257	377	200.19	383	300	✓		✓	✓			4	9	
Total		90																				
TGV2N: Double Deck	1994-96	45	2	3	4	1	10	197	348	545	200.19	380	300	✓			✓		8x1100 =8800	4	9	
PBKA	From 1997	27	2	3	5	-	10	120	257	377	200.19	385	300	✓	✓	✓	✓		8x1100 =8800	4	9	8

(1) Catering service car with buffet
(2) Number of traction motors multiplied by kW
(3) The postal fleet consists of five half-sets; carrying capacity is 61 tonnes of post in pallets.
(4) Ownership is: 11 BR (European Passenger Services), 16 SNCF and four SNCB
(5) Ownership European Passenger Services
(6) Ownership RENFE
(7) There are four seating grades: 30 Club, eight conference room, 78 Preferenta and 31 Tourist
(8) Ownership is: three German Railways (DB), four Netherlands Railways (NS), 11 SNCB and nine SNCF

DECELERATION TABLES

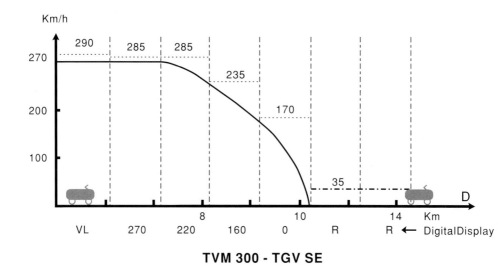

TVM 300 - TGV SE

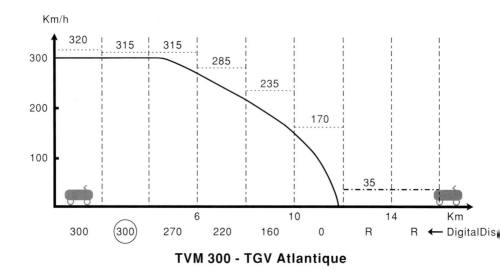

TVM 300 - TGV Atlantique

———— Manual braking curve   .... Speed limit   (xxx) Flashing sign in cab

110

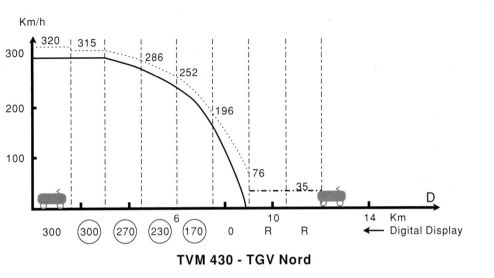

TVM 430 - TGV Nord

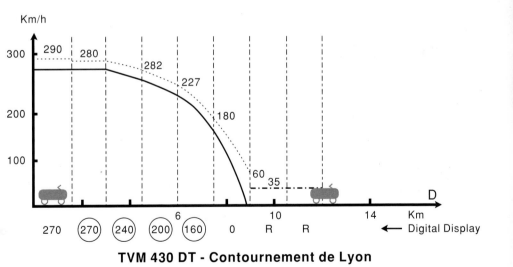

TVM 430 DT - Contournement de Lyon

—— Manual braking curve .... Speed limit (xxx) Flashing sign in cab

111

TRAINSET AND VEHICLE NUMBERING

Unit Number	Paris Sud Est Two-Voltage	Paris Sud Est Three-Voltage	Postal	Atlantique	Réseau Two-Voltage	Réseau Three-Voltage
	M+8R+M	M+8R+M	M+8R+M	M+10R+M	M+8R+M	M+8R+M
	1 - 102	110 - 118	1 - 5	301 - 405	501 - 550	4501 - 4530
M1/M2	23001-23204	33001-33018	923001-923005	24001-24210	28001-28100	380001-380061
R1	123001-123102	133110-133118	912301-912303	241301-241405	281501-281550	3845011-384530
R2	223001-223102	233110-233118	922301-922303	242301-242405	282501-282550	3845012-384530
R3	323001-323102	333110-333118	932301-932303	243301-243405	283501-283550	3845013-384530
R4	423001-423102	433110-433118	942301-942303	244301-244405	284501-284550	3845014-384530
R5	523001-523102	533110-533118	952301-952302	245301-245405	285501-285550	3845015-384530
R6	623001-623102	633110-633118	962301-962302	246301-246405	286501-286550	3845016-384530
R7	723001-723102	733110-733118	972301-972302	247301-247405	287501-287550	3845017-384530
R8	823001-823102	833110-833118	982301-982302	248301-248405	288501-288550	3845018-384530
R9	-	-	-	249301-249405	-	-
R10	-	-	-	240301-240405	-	-

TGV test coach No 230001 'Mélusine'   M (motrice = power car) R (remorque = trailer)

In the PSE fleet power cars are numbered from 23001 (Two-Voltage Units) and 33001 (Three-Voltage Units). Power cars (M1/M2) are in pairs - 23001 and 23002 will be formed in unit No 1, 23003 and 23004 in unit No 2 and so on. The number of each vehicle is preceded by the letters TGV and, for the trailers, symbols and identification characteristics according to whether the vehicle is First, Second Class, Bar etc. The trailers bear a six-figure number. The first one from the left (1-8) shows the position of the trailer from the first power car M1 in the set. The following two figures indicate that it belongs to a Two or Three-Voltage set. The last three to the right indicate the number of the set carried at each end on the power car units. Postal, Atlantique and Réseau numbering is based on the same system